A PASSAGE TO INDIA

E.M. Forster

EDITORIAL DIRECTOR Justin Kestler
EXECUTIVE EDITOR Ben Florman

SERIES EDITORS Boomie Aglietti, John Crowther, Justin Kestler
PRODUCTION Christian Lorentzen

WRITER Laura Heffernan
EDITORS Matt Blanchard, John Crowther

This edition published by Spark Publishing

Spark Publishing
A Division of SparkNotes LLC
120 Fifth Avenue, 8th Floor
New York, NY 10011

02 03 04 05 SN 9 8 7 6 5 4 3 2 1

Please send all comments and questions or report errors to
feedback@sparknotes.com.

Library of Congress information available upon request

Printed and bound in the United States

RRD-C

ISBN 1-58663-819-X

INTRODUCTION: STOPPING TO BUY SPARKNOTES ON A SNOWY EVENING

Whose words these are you *think* you know.
Your paper's due tomorrow, though;
We're glad to see you stopping here
To get some help before you go.

Lost your course? You'll find it here.
Face tests and essays without fear.
Between the words, good grades at stake:
Get great results throughout the year.

Once school bells caused your heart to quake
As teachers circled each mistake.
Use SparkNotes and no longer weep,
Ace every single test you take.

Yes, books are lovely, dark, and deep,
But only what you grasp you keep,
With hours to go before you sleep,
With hours to go before you sleep.

CONTENTS

CONTEXT

EDWARD MORGAN FORSTER WAS BORN into a comfortable London family in 1879. His father, an architect, died when Forster was very young, leaving the boy to be raised by his mother and great-aunt. Forster proved to be a bright student, and he went on to attend Cambridge University, graduating in 1901. He spent much of the next decade traveling and living abroad, dividing his time between working as a journalist and writing short stories and novels.

Many of Forster's observations and experiences from this time figure in his fiction, most notably *A Room with a View* (1908), which chronicles the experiences of a group of English people vacationing in Italy. Two years after *A Room with a View,* the novel *Howards End* (1910), in which Forster criticized the class divisions and prejudices of Edwardian England, solidified his reputation as a social critic and a master of incisively observational fiction.

Long before Forster first visited India, he had already gained a vivid picture of its people and places from a young Indian Muslim named Syed Ross Masood, whom Forster began tutoring in England starting in 1906. Forster and Masood became very close, and Masood introduced Forster to several of his Indian friends. Echoes of the friendship between the two can be seen in the characters of Fielding and Aziz in *A Passage to India.* By the time Forster first visited India, in 1912, the Englishman was well prepared for his travels throughout the country.

At the time of Forster's visit, the British government had been officially ruling India since 1858, after the failed Sepoy Rebellion in 1857, in which Indians attempted to regain rule from the British East India Company. The East India Company, a privately owned trading concern, had been gaining financial and political power in India since the seventeenth century. By the time of Forster's visit, Britain's control over India was complete: English governors headed each province and were responsible to Parliament. Though England had promised the Indian people a role in government in exchange for their aid during World War I, India did not win independence until three decades later, in 1949.

Forster spent time with both Englishmen and Indians during his visit, and he quickly found he preferred the company of the latter.

He was troubled by the racial oppression and deep cultural misunderstandings that divided the Indian people and the British colonists, or, as they are called in *A Passage to India*, Anglo-Indians. The prevailing attitude among the British in India was that the colonists were assuming the "white man's burden"—novelist Rudyard Kipling's phrase—of governing the country, because the Indians could not handle the responsibility themselves. Forster, a homosexual living in a society and era largely unsympathetic to his lifestyle, had long experienced prejudice and misunderstanding firsthand. It is no surprise, then, that Forster felt sympathetic toward the Indian side of the colonial argument. Indeed, Forster became a lifelong advocate for tolerance and understanding among people of different social classes, races, and backgrounds.

Forster began writing *A Passage to India* in 1913, just after his first visit to India. The novel was not revised and completed, however, until well after his second stay in India, in 1921, when he served as secretary to the Maharajah of Dewas State Senior. Published in 1924, *A Passage to India* examines the racial misunderstandings and cultural hypocrisies that characterized the complex interactions between Indians and the English toward the end of the British occupation of India.

Forster's style is marked by his sympathy for his characters, his ability to see more than one side of an argument or story, and his fondness for simple, symbolic tales that neatly encapsulate large-scale problems and conditions. These tendencies are all evident in *A Passage to India*, which was immediately acclaimed as Forster's masterpiece upon its publication. It is a traditional social and political novel, unconcerned with the technical innovation of some of Forster's modernist contemporaries such as Gertrude Stein or T.S. Eliot. *A Passage to India* is concerned, however, with representing the chaos of modern human experience through patterns of imagery and form. In this regard, Forster's novel is similar to modernist works of the same time period, such as James Joyce's *Ulysses* (1922) and Virginia Woolf's *Mrs. Dalloway* (1925).

A Passage to India was the last in a string of Forster's novels in which his craft improved markedly with each new work. After the novel's publication, however, Forster never again attained the level of craft or the depth of observation that characterized his early work. In his later life, he contented himself primarily with writing critical essays and lectures, most notably *Aspects of the Novel* (1927). In 1946, Forster accepted a fellowship at Cambridge, where he remained until his death in 1970.

PLOT OVERVIEW

TWO ENGLISHWOMEN, THE YOUNG Miss Adela Quested and the elderly Mrs. Moore, travel to India. Adela expects to become engaged to Mrs. Moore's son, Ronny, a British magistrate in the Indian city of Chandrapore. Adela and Mrs. Moore each hope to see the real India during their visit, rather than cultural institutions imported by the British.

At the same time, Aziz, a young Muslim doctor in India, is increasingly frustrated by the poor treatment he receives at the hands of the English. Aziz is especially annoyed with Major Callendar, the civil surgeon, who has a tendency to summon Aziz for frivolous reasons in the middle of dinner. Aziz and two of his educated friends, Hamidullah and Mahmoud Ali, hold a lively conversation about whether or not an Indian can be friends with an Englishman in India. That night, Mrs. Moore and Aziz happen to run into each other while exploring a local mosque, and the two become friendly. Aziz is moved and surprised that an English person would treat him like a friend.

Mr. Turton, the collector who governs Chandrapore, hosts a party so that Adela and Mrs. Moore may have the opportunity to meet some of the more prominent and wealthy Indians in the city. At the event, which proves to be rather awkward, Adela meets Cyril Fielding, the principal of the government college in Chandrapore. Fielding, impressed with Adela's open friendliness to the Indians, invites her and Mrs. Moore to tea with him and the Hindu professor Godbole. At Adela's request, Fielding invites Aziz to tea as well.

At the tea, Aziz and Fielding immediately become friendly, and the afternoon is overwhelmingly pleasant until Ronny Heaslop arrives and rudely interrupts the party. Later that evening, Adela tells Ronny that she has decided not to marry him. But that night, the two are in a car accident together, and the excitement of the event causes Adela to change her mind about the marriage.

Not long afterward, Aziz organizes an expedition to the nearby Marabar Caves for those who attended Fielding's tea. Fielding and Professor Godbole miss the train to Marabar, so Aziz continues on alone with the two ladies, Adela and Mrs. Moore. Inside one of the caves, Mrs. Moore is unnerved by the enclosed space, which is crowded with Aziz's retinue, and by the uncanny echo that seems to translate every sound she makes into the noise "boum."

Aziz, Adela, and a guide go on to the higher caves while Mrs. Moore waits below. Adela, suddenly realizing that she does not love Ronny, asks Aziz whether he has more than one wife—a question he considers offensive. Aziz storms off into a cave, and when he returns, Adela is gone. Aziz scolds the guide for losing Adela, and the guide runs away. Aziz finds Adela's broken field-glasses and heads down the hill. Back at the picnic site, Aziz finds Fielding waiting for him. Aziz is unconcerned to learn that Adela has hastily taken a car back to Chandrapore, as he is overjoyed to see Fielding. Back in Chandrapore, however, Aziz is unexpectedly arrested. He is charged with attempting to rape Adela Quested while she was in the caves, a charge based on a claim Adela herself has made.

Fielding, believing Aziz to be innocent, angers all of British India by joining the Indians in Aziz's defense. In the weeks before the trial, the racial tensions between the Indians and the English flare up considerably. Mrs. Moore is distracted and miserable because of her memory of the echo in the cave and because of her impatience with the upcoming trial. Adela is emotional and ill; she too seems to suffer from an echo in her mind. Ronny is fed up with Mrs. Moore's lack of support for Adela, and it is agreed that Mrs. Moore will return to England earlier than planned. Mrs. Moore dies on the voyage back to England, but not before she realizes that there is no "real India"—but rather a complex multitude of different Indias.

At Aziz's trial, Adela, under oath, is questioned about what happened in the caves. Shockingly, she declares that she has made a mistake: Aziz is not the person or thing that attacked her in the cave. Aziz is set free, and Fielding escorts Adela to the Government College, where she spends the next several weeks. Fielding begins to respect Adela, recognizing her bravery in standing against her peers to pronounce Aziz innocent. Ronny breaks off his engagement to Adela, and she returns to England.

Aziz, however, is angry that Fielding would befriend Adela after she nearly ruined Aziz's life, and the friendship between the two men suffers as a consequence. Then Fielding sails for a visit to England. Aziz declares that he is done with the English and that he intends to move to a place where he will not have to encounter them.

Two years later, Aziz has become the chief doctor to the Rajah of Mau, a Hindu region several hundred miles from Chandrapore. He has heard that Fielding married Adela shortly after returning to

England. Aziz now virulently hates all English people. One day, walking through an old temple with his three children, he encounters Fielding and his brother-in-law. Aziz is surprised to learn that the brother-in-law's name is Ralph Moore; it turns out that Fielding married not Adela Quested, but Stella Moore, Mrs. Moore's daughter from her second marriage.

Aziz befriends Ralph. After he accidentally runs his rowboat into Fielding's, Aziz renews his friendship with Fielding as well. The two men go for a final ride together before Fielding leaves, during which Aziz tells Fielding that once the English are out of India, the two will be able to be friends. Fielding asks why they cannot be friends now, when they both want to be, but the sky and the earth seem to say "No, not yet. . . . No, not there."

Character List

Dr. Aziz   An intelligent, emotional Indian doctor in Chandrapore. Aziz attempts to make friends with Adela Quested, Mrs. Moore, and Cyril Fielding. Later, Adela falsely accuses Aziz of attempted rape after an expedition to the Marabar Caves, but the charges are dropped after Adela's testimony at the trial. Aziz enjoys writing and reciting poetry. He has three children; his wife died several years before the beginning of the novel.

Cyril Fielding The principal of the government college near Chandrapore. Fielding is an independent man who believes in educating the Indians to be individuals—a much more sympathetic attitude toward the native population than that held by most English in India. Fielding befriends Dr. Aziz, taking the doctor's side against the rest of the English in Chandrapore when Aziz is accused of attempting to rape Adela Quested.

Miss Adela Quested A young, intelligent, inquisitive, but somewhat repressed Englishwoman. Adela travels to India with Mrs. Moore in order to decide whether or not to marry Mrs. Moore's son Ronny. Miss Quested begins with an openminded desire to get to know Indians and see the real India. Later, she falsely accuses Aziz of attempting to rape her in the Marabar Caves.

Mrs. Moore An elderly Englishwoman who voyages to India with Adela Quested. Mrs. Moore wishes to see the country and hopes that Adela will marry her son Ronny. Mrs. Moore befriends Dr. Aziz, as she feels some spiritual connection with him. She has an unsettling experience with the bizarre echoes in the Marabar Caves, which cause her to feel a sense of dread, especially about human relationships. Mrs. Moore hurries back to England, and she dies at sea during the journey.

Ronny Heaslop Mrs. Moore's son, the magistrate at
    Chandrapore. Ronny, though well educated and open-
    minded at heart, has become prejudiced and intolerant
    of Indians ever since he moved to India—as is standard
    for most Englishmen serving there. Ronny is briefly
    engaged to Adela Quested, though he does not appear
    particularly passionate about her.

Mr. Turton The collector, the man who governs Chandrapore. Mr.
    Turton is officious and stern, though more tactful than
    his wife.

Mrs. Turton Turton's wife. In her interactions with Indians, Mrs.
    Turton embodies the novel's stereotype of the snobby,
    rude, and prejudiced English colonial wife.

Mr. McBryde The superintendent of police in Chandrapore, who
    has an elaborate theory that he claims explains the
    inferiority of dark-skinned races to light-skinned ones.
    McBryde, though condescending, actually shows more
    tolerance toward Indians than most English do. Not
    surprisingly, he and Fielding are friendly acquain-
    tances. McBryde himself stands up against the
    group mentality of the English at Chandrapore when
    he divorces his wife after having an affair with
    Miss Derek.

Major Callendar The civil surgeon at Chandrapore, Dr. Aziz's
    superior. Major Callendar is a boastful, cruel,
    intolerant, and ridiculous man.

Professor Godbole A Brahman Hindu who teaches at Fielding's
    college. Godbole is very spiritual and reluctant to
    become involved in human affairs.

Hamidullah Dr. Aziz's uncle and friend. Hamidullah, who was
    educated at Cambridge, believes that friendship
    between the English and Indians is more likely possible
    in England than in India. Hamidullah was a close
    friend of Fielding before Fielding and Aziz met.

CHARACTER LIST

Mahmoud Ali A lawyer friend of Dr. Aziz who is deeply pessimistic about the English.

The Nawab Bahadur The leading loyalist in Chandrapore. The Nawab Bahadur is wealthy, generous, and faithful to the English. After Aziz's trial, however, he gives up his title in protest.

Dr. Panna Lal A low-born Hindu doctor and Aziz's rival. Dr. Panna Lal intends to testify against Aziz at the trial, but he begs forgiveness after Aziz is set free.

Stella Moore Mrs. Moore's daughter from her second marriage. Stella marries Fielding toward the end of the novel.

Ralph Moore Mrs. Moore's son from her second marriage, a sensitive young man.

Miss Derek A young Englishwoman who works for a wealthy Indian family and often steals their car. Miss Derek is easygoing and has a fine sense of humor, but many of the English at Chandrapore resent her, considering her presence unseemly.

Amritrao The lawyer who defends Aziz at his trial. Amritrao is a highly anti-British man.

ANALYSIS OF MAJOR CHARACTERS

DR. AZIZ

Aziz seems to be a mess of extremes and contradictions, an embodiment of Forster's notion of the "muddle" of India. Aziz is impetuous and flighty, changing opinions and preoccupations quickly and without warning, from one moment to the next. His moods swing back and forth between extremes, from childlike elation one minute to utter despair the next. Aziz even seems capable of shifting careers and talents, serving as both physician and poet during the course of *A Passage to India*. Aziz's somewhat youthful qualities, as evidenced by a sense of humor that leans toward practical joking, are offset by his attitude of irony toward his English superiors.

Forster, though not blatantly stereotyping, encourages us to see many of Aziz's characteristics as characteristics of Indians in general. Aziz, like many of his friends, dislikes blunt honesty and directness, preferring to communicate through confidences, feelings underlying words, and indirect speech. Aziz has a sense that much of morality is really social code. He therefore feels no moral compunction about visiting prostitutes or reading Fielding's private mail—both because his intentions are good and because he knows he will not be caught. Instead of living by merely social codes, Aziz guides his action through a code that is nearly religious, such as we see in his extreme hospitality. Moreover, Aziz, like many of the other Indians, struggles with the problem of the English in India. On the one hand, he appreciates some of the modernizing influences that the West has brought to India; on the other, he feels that the presence of the English degrades and oppresses his people.

Despite his contradictions, Aziz is a genuinely affectionate character, and his affection is often based on intuited connections, as with Mrs. Moore and Fielding. Though Forster holds up Aziz's capacity for imaginative sympathy as a good trait, we see that this imaginativeness can also betray Aziz. The deep offense Aziz feels toward Fielding in the aftermath of his trial stems from fiction and misinterpreted intuition. Aziz does not stop to evaluate facts, but rather follows his heart to the exclusion of all other methods—an approach that is sometimes wrong.

Many critics have contended that Forster portrays Aziz and many of the other Indian characters unflatteringly. Indeed, though the author is certainly sympathetic to the Indians, he does sometimes present them as incompetent, subservient, or childish. These somewhat valid critiques call into question the realism of Forster's novel, but they do not, on the whole, corrupt his exploration of the possibility of friendly relations between Indians and Englishmen—arguably the central concern of the novel.

CYRIL FIELDING

Of all the characters in the novel, Fielding is clearly the most associated with Forster himself. Among the Englishmen in Chandrapore, Fielding is far and away most the successful at developing and sustaining relationships with native Indians. Though he is an educator, he is less comfortable in teacher-student interaction than he is in one-on-one conversation with another individual. This latter style serves as Forster's model of liberal humanism—Forster and Fielding treat the world as a group of individuals who can connect through mutual respect, courtesy, and intelligence.

Fielding, in these viewpoints, presents the main threat to the mentality of the English in India. He educates Indians as individuals, engendering a movement of free thought that has the potential to destabilize English colonial power. Furthermore, Fielding has little patience for the racial categorization that is so central to the English grip on India. He honors his friendship with Aziz over any alliance with members of his own race—a reshuffling of allegiances that threatens the solidarity of the English. Finally, Fielding "travels light," as he puts it: he does not believe in marriage, but favors friendship instead. As such, Fielding implicitly questions the domestic conventions upon which the Englishmen's sense of "Englishness" is founded. Fielding refuses to sentimentalize domestic England or to venerate the role of the wife or mother—a far cry from the other Englishmen, who put Adela on a pedestal after the incident at the caves.

Fielding's character changes in the aftermath of Aziz's trial. He becomes jaded about the Indians as well as the English. His English sensibilities, such as his need for proportion and reason, become more prominent and begin to grate against Aziz's Indian sensibilities. By the end of *A Passage to India,* Forster seems to identify with Fielding less. Whereas Aziz remains a likable, if flawed, character until the end of the novel, Fielding becomes less likable in his increasing identification and sameness with the English.

ADELA QUESTED

Adela arrives in India with Mrs. Moore, and, fittingly, her character develops in parallel to Mrs. Moore's. Adela, like the elder English-woman, is an individualist and an educated free thinker. These tendencies lead her, just as they lead Mrs. Moore, to question the standard behaviors of the English toward the Indians. Adela's tendency to question standard practices with frankness makes her resistant to being labeled—and therefore resistant to marrying Ronny and being labeled a typical colonial English wife. Both Mrs. Moore and Adela hope to see the "real India" rather than an arranged tourist version. However, whereas Mrs. Moore's desire is bolstered by a genuine interest in and affection for Indians, Adela appears to want to see the "real India" simply on intellectual grounds. She puts her mind to the task, but not her heart—and therefore never connects with Indians.

Adela's experience at the Marabar Caves causes her to undergo a crisis of rationalism against spiritualism. While Adela's character changes greatly in the several days after her alleged assault, her testimony at the trial represents a return of the old Adela, with the sole difference that she is plagued by doubt in a way she was not originally. Adela begins to sense that her assault, and the echo that haunts her afterward, are representative of something outside the scope of her normal rational comprehension. She is pained by her inability to articulate her experience. She finds she has no purpose in—nor love for—India, and suddenly fears that she is unable to love anyone. Adela is filled with the realization of the damage she has done to Aziz and others, yet she feels paralyzed, unable to remedy the wrongs she has done. Nonetheless, Adela selflessly endures her difficult fate after the trial—a course of action that wins her a friend in Fielding, who sees her as a brave woman rather than a traitor to her race.

MRS. MOORE

As a character, Mrs. Moore serves a double function in *A Passage to India,* operating on two different planes. She is initially a literal character, but as the novel progresses she becomes more a symbolic presence. On the literal level, Mrs. Moore is a good-hearted, religious, elderly woman with mystical leanings. The initial days of her visit to India are successful, as she connects with India and Indians on an intuitive level. Whereas Adela is overly cerebral, Mrs. Moore relies successfully on her heart to make connections during her visit. Furthermore, on the literal level, Mrs. Moore's character has human limitations: her experience at Marabar renders her apathetic and even somewhat mean, to the degree that she simply leaves India without bothering to testify to Aziz's innocence or to oversee Ronny and Adela's wedding.

After her departure, however, Mrs. Moore exists largely on a symbolic level. Though she herself has human flaws, she comes to symbolize an ideally spiritual and race-blind openness that Forster sees as a solution to the problems in India. Mrs. Moore's name becomes closely associated with Hinduism, especially the Hindu tenet of the oneness and unity of all living things. This symbolic side to Mrs. Moore might even make her the heroine of the novel, the only English person able to closely connect with the Hindu vision of unity. Nonetheless, Mrs. Moore's literal actions—her sudden abandonment of India—make her less than heroic.

RONNY HEASLOP

Ronny's character does not change much over the course of the novel; instead, Forster's emphasis is on the change that happened before the novel begins, when Ronny first arrived in India. Both Mrs. Moore and Adela note the difference between the Ronny they knew in England and the Ronny of British India. Forster uses Ronny's character and the changes he has undergone as a sort of case study, an exploration of the restrictions that the English colonials' herd mentality imposes on individual personalities. All of Ronny's previously individual tastes are effectively dumbed down to meet group standards. He devalues his intelligence and learning from England in favor of the "wisdom" gained by years of experience in India. The open-minded attitude with which he has been brought up has been replaced by a suspicion of Indians. In short,

Ronny's tastes, opinions, and even his manner of speaking are no longer his own, but those of older, ostensibly wiser British Indian officials. This kind of group thinking is what ultimately causes Ronny to clash with both Adela and his mother, Mrs. Moore.

Nonetheless, Ronny is not the worst of the English in India, and Forster is somewhat sympathetic in his portrayal of him. Ronny's ambition to rise in the ranks of British India has not completely destroyed his natural goodness, but merely perverted it. Ronny cares about his job and the Indians with whom he works, if only to the extent that they, in turn, reflect upon him. Forster presents Ronny's failing as the fault of the colonial system, not his own.

CHARACTER ANALYSIS

THEMES, MOTIFS & SYMBOLS

THEMES

Themes are the fundamental and often universal ideas explored in a literary work.

THE DIFFICULTY OF ENGLISH-INDIAN FRIENDSHIP

A Passage to India begins and ends by posing the question of whether it is possible for an Englishman and an Indian to ever be friends, at least within the context of British colonialism. Forster uses this question as a framework to explore the general issue of Britain's political control of India on a more personal level, through the friendship between Aziz and Fielding. At the beginning of the novel, Aziz is scornful of the English, wishing only to consider them comically or ignore them completely. Yet the intuitive connection Aziz feels with Mrs. Moore in the mosque opens him to the possibility of friendship with Fielding. Through the first half of the novel, Fielding and Aziz represent a positive model of liberal humanism: Forster suggests that British rule in India could be successful and respectful if only English and Indians treated each other as Fielding and Aziz treat each other—as worthy individuals who connect through frankness, intelligence, and good will.

Yet in the aftermath of the novel's climax—Adela's accusation that Aziz attempted to assault her and her subsequent disavowal of this accusation at the trial—Aziz and Fielding's friendship falls apart. The strains on their relationship are external in nature, as Aziz and Fielding both suffer from the tendencies of their cultures. Aziz tends to let his imagination run away with him and to let suspicion harden into a grudge. Fielding suffers from an English literalism and rationalism that blind him to Aziz's true feelings and make Fielding too stilted to reach out to Aziz through conversations or letters. Furthermore, their respective Indian and English communities pull them apart through their mutual stereotyping. As we see at the end of the novel, even the landscape of India seems to oppress their friendship. Forster's final vision of the possibility of English-

Indian friendship is a pessimistic one, yet it is qualified by the possibility of friendship on English soil, or after the liberation of India. As the landscape itself seems to imply at the end of the novel, such a friendship may be possible eventually, but "not yet."

THE UNITY OF ALL LIVING THINGS

Though the main characters of *A Passage to India* are generally Christian or Muslim, Hinduism also plays a large thematic role in the novel. The aspect of Hinduism with which Forster is particularly concerned is the religion's ideal of all living things, from the lowliest to the highest, united in love as one. This vision of the universe appears to offer redemption to India through mysticism, as individual differences disappear into a peaceful collectivity that does not recognize hierarchies. Individual blame and intrigue is forgone in favor of attention to higher, spiritual matters. Professor Godbole, the most visible Hindu in the novel, is Forster's mouthpiece for this idea of the unity of all living things. Godbole alone remains aloof from the drama of the plot, refraining from taking sides by recognizing that all are implicated in the evil of Marabar. Mrs. Moore, also, shows openness to this aspect of Hinduism. Though she is a Christian, her experience of India has made her dissatisfied with what she perceives as the smallness of Christianity. Mrs. Moore appears to feel a great sense of connection with all living creatures, as evidenced by her respect for the wasp in her bedroom.

Yet, through Mrs. Moore, Forster also shows that the vision of the oneness of all living things can be terrifying. As we see in Mrs. Moore's experience with the echo that negates everything into "boum" in Marabar, such oneness provides unity but also makes all elements of the universe one and the same—a realization that, it is implied, ultimately kills Mrs. Moore. Godbole is not troubled by the idea that negation is an inevitable result when all things come together as one. Mrs. Moore, however, loses interest in the world of relationships after envisioning this lack of distinctions as a horror. Moreover, though Forster generally endorses the Hindu idea of the oneness of all living things, he also suggests that there may be inherent problems with it. Even Godbole, for example, seems to recognize that something—if only a stone—must be left out of the vision of oneness if the vision is to cohere. This problem of exclusion is, in a sense, merely another manifestation of the individual difference and hierarchy that Hinduism promises to overcome.

THE "MUDDLE" OF INDIA

Forster takes great care to strike a distinction between the ideas of "muddle" and "mystery" in *A Passage to India*. "Muddle" has connotations of dangerous and disorienting disorder, whereas "mystery" suggests a mystical, orderly plan by a spiritual force that is greater than man. Fielding, who acts as Forster's primary mouthpiece in the novel, admits that India is a "muddle," while figures such as Mrs. Moore and Godbole view India as a mystery. The muddle that is India in the novel appears to work from the ground up: the very landscape and architecture of the countryside is formless, and the natural life of plants and animals defies identification. This muddled quality to the environment is mirrored in the makeup of India's native population, which is mixed into a muddle of different religious, ethnic, linguistic, and regional groups.

The muddle of India disorients Adela the most; indeed, the events at the Marabar Caves that trouble her so much can be seen as a manifestation of this muddle. By the end of the novel, we are still not sure what actually has happened in the caves. Forster suggests that Adela's feelings about Ronny become externalized and muddled in the caves, and that she suddenly experiences these feelings as something outside of her. The muddle of India also affects Aziz and Fielding's friendship, as their good intentions are derailed by the chaos of cross-cultural signals.

Though Forster is sympathetic to India and Indians in the novel, his overwhelming depiction of India as a muddle matches the manner in which many Western writers of his day treated the East in their works. As the noted critic Edward Said has pointed out, these authors' "orientalizing" of the East made Western logic and capability appear self-evident, and, by extension, portrayed the West's domination of the East as reasonable or even necessary.

THE NEGLIGENCE OF BRITISH COLONIAL GOVERNMENT

Though *A Passage to India* is in many ways a highly symbolic, or even mystical, text, it also aims to be a realistic documentation of the attitudes of British colonial officials in India. Forster spends large sections of the novel characterizing different typical attitudes the English hold toward the Indians whom they control. Forster's satire is most harsh toward Englishwomen, whom the author depicts as overwhelmingly racist, self-righteous, and viciously condescending to the native population. Some of the Englishmen in the novel are as nasty as the women, but Forster more often identifies Englishmen as men who, though condescending and unable to relate to Indians on an individual level, are largely well-meaning and invested in their jobs. For all Forster's criticism of the British manner of governing India, however, he does not appear to question the right of the British Empire to rule India. He suggests that the British would be well served by becoming kinder and more sympathetic to the Indians with whom they live, but he does not suggest that the British should abandon India outright. Even this lesser critique is never overtly stated in the novel, but implied through biting satire.

MOTIFS

Motifs are recurring structures, contrasts, or literary devices that can help to develop and inform the text's major themes.

THE ECHO

The echo begins at the Marabar Caves: first Mrs. Moore and then Adela hear the echo and are haunted by it in the weeks to come. The echo's sound is "boum"—a sound it returns regardless of what noise or utterance is originally made. This negation of difference embodies the frightening flip side of the seemingly positive Hindu vision of the oneness and unity of all living things. If all people and things become the same thing, then no distinction can be made between good and evil. No value system can exist. The echo plagues Mrs. Moore until her death, causing her to abandon her beliefs and cease to care about human relationships. Adela, however, ultimately escapes the echo by using its message of impersonality to help her realize Aziz's innocence.

EASTERN AND WESTERN ARCHITECTURE

Forster spends time detailing both Eastern and Western architecture in *A Passage to India*. Three architectural structures—though one is naturally occurring—provide the outline for the book's three sections, "Mosque," "Caves," and "Temple." Forster presents the aesthetics of Eastern and Western structures as indicative of the differences of the respective cultures as a whole. In India, architecture is confused and formless: interiors blend into exterior gardens, earth and buildings compete with each other, and structures appear unfinished or drab. As such, Indian architecture mirrors the muddle of India itself and what Forster sees as the Indians' characteristic inattention to form and logic. Occasionally, however, Forster takes a positive view of Indian architecture. The mosque in Part I and temple in Part III represent the promise of Indian openness, mysticism, and friendship. Western architecture, meanwhile, is described during Fielding's stop in Venice on his way to England. Venice's structures, which Fielding sees as representative of Western architecture in general, honor form and proportion and complement the earth on which they are built. Fielding reads in this architecture the self-evident correctness of Western reason—an order that, he laments, his Indian friends would not recognize or appreciate.

GODBOLE'S SONG
At the end of Fielding's tea party, Godbole sings for the English visitors a Hindu song, in which a milkmaid pleads for God to come to her or to her people. The song's refrain of "Come! come" recurs throughout *A Passage to India*, mirroring the appeal for the entire country of salvation from something greater than itself. After the song, Godbole admits that God never comes to the milkmaid. The song greatly disheartens Mrs. Moore, setting the stage for her later spiritual apathy, her simultaneous awareness of a spiritual presence and lack of confidence in spiritualism as a redeeming force. Godbole seemingly intends his song as a message or lesson that recognition of the potential existence of a God figure can bring the world together and erode differences—after all, Godbole himself sings the part of a young milkmaid. Forster uses the refrain of Godbole's song, "Come! come," to suggest that India's redemption is yet to come.

SYMBOLS

Symbols are objects, characters, figures, or colors used to represent abstract ideas or concepts.

THE MARABAR CAVES
The Marabar Caves represent all that is alien about nature. The caves are older than anything else on the earth and embody nothingness and emptiness—a literal void in the earth. They defy both English and Indians to act as guides to them, and their strange beauty and menace unsettles visitors. The caves' alien quality also has the power to make visitors such as Mrs. Moore and Adela confront parts of themselves or the universe that they have not previously recognized. The all-reducing echo of the caves causes Mrs.

Moore to see the darker side of her spirituality—a waning commitment to the world of relationships and a growing ambivalence about God. Adela confronts the shame and embarrassment of her realization that she and Ronny are not actually attracted to each other, and that she might be attracted to no one. In this sense, the caves both destroy meaning, in reducing all utterances to the same sound, and expose or narrate the unspeakable, the aspects of the universe that the caves' visitors have not yet considered.

THE GREEN BIRD

Just after Adela and Ronny agree for the first time, in Chapter VII, to break off their engagement, they notice a green bird sitting in the tree above them. Neither of them can positively identify the bird. For Adela, the bird symbolizes the unidentifiable quality of all of India: just when she thinks she can understand any aspect of India, that aspect changes or disappears. In this sense, the green bird symbolizes the muddle of India. In another capacity, the bird points to a different tension between the English and Indians. The English are obsessed with knowledge, literalness, and naming, and they use these tools as a means of gaining and maintaining power. The Indians, in contrast, are more attentive to nuance, undertone, and the emotions behind words. While the English insist on labeling things, the Indians recognize that labels can blind one to important details and differences. The unidentifiable green bird suggests the incompatibility of the English obsession with classification and order with the shifting quality of India itself—the land is, in fact, a "hundred Indias" that defy labeling and understanding.

THE WASP

The wasp appears several times in *A Passage to India,* usually in conjunction with the Hindu vision of the oneness of all living things. The wasp is usually depicted as the lowest creature the Hindus incorporate into their vision of universal unity. Mrs. Moore is closely associated with the wasp, as she finds one in her room and is gently appreciative of it. Her peaceful regard for the wasp signifies her own openness to the Hindu idea of collectivity, and to the mysticism and indefinable quality of India in general. However, as the wasp is the lowest creature that the Hindus visualize, it also represents the limits of the Hindu vision. The vision is not a panacea, but merely a possibility for unity and understanding in India.

Summary & Analysis

Part I, Chapters I–III

Summary: Chapter I

The city of Chandrapore, apart from the nearby Marabar Caves, is unextraordinary. The small, dirty city sits next to the River Ganges. Slightly inland from the city, near the railway station, lie the plain, sensible buildings of the British colonials. From the vantage point of these buildings, Chandrapore appears lovely because its unattractive parts are obscured by tropical vegetation. Newcomers, in order to lose their romantic image of the city, must be driven down to the city itself. The British buildings and the rest of Chandrapore are connected only by the Indian sky. The sky dominates the whole landscape, except for the Marabar Hills, which contain the only extraordinary part of Chandrapore—the Marabar Caves.

Summary: Chapter II

Dr. Aziz, an Indian Muslim, arrives late to his friend Hamidullah's house, where Hamidullah and Mahmoud Ali are engaged in a debate over whether it is possible for an Indian and an Englishman to be friends. Hamidullah, who studied at Cambridge when he was young, contends that such a cross-cultural friendship is possible in England. The men agree that Englishmen in India all become insufferable within two years and all Englishwomen within six months. Aziz prefers to happily ignore the English.

Hamidullah takes Aziz behind the purdah (the screen that separates women from public interaction) to chat with his wife. Hamidullah's wife scolds Aziz for not having remarried after the death of his wife. Aziz, however, is happy with his life, and sees his three children at his mother-in-law's house often.

The men sit down to dinner along with Mohammed Latif, a poor, lazy relative of Hamidullah. Aziz recites poetry for the men, and they listen happily, feeling momentarily that India is one. Poetry in India is a public event.

During dinner, Aziz receives a summons from his superior, Major Callendar, the civil surgeon. Annoyed, Aziz bicycles away to

Callendar's bungalow. When Aziz's bicycle tire deflates, he hires a tonga (a small pony-drawn vehicle) and finally arrives at Callendar's house to find that the major has gone and left no message. Furthermore, as Aziz is speaking with a servant on the porch, Mrs. Callendar and her friend Mrs. Lesley rudely take Aziz's hired tonga for their own use.

Aziz decides to walk home. On the way, he stops at his favorite mosque. To Aziz, the mosque, with its beautiful architecture, is a symbol of the truth of Islam and love. Aziz imagines building his own mosque with an inscription for his tomb addressing "those who have secretly understood my heart."

Aziz suddenly notices an Englishwoman in the mosque and yells at her angrily, for she is trespassing in a holy place for Muslims. The woman is humble, however, and explains that she removed her shoes upon entering and that she realizes that God is present in the mosque. Aziz is impressed. The woman introduces herself as Mrs. Moore. She is visiting her son, Ronny Heaslop, the city magistrate.

Aziz and Mrs. Moore discover that they each have two sons and a daughter. Aziz senses Mrs. Moore's friendly sympathy toward him—a sense confirmed when Mrs. Moore speaks candidly of her distaste for Mrs. Callendar, the major's wife. Because Mrs. Moore is intuitively able to sense whom she likes and does not like, Aziz pronounces her an Oriental. Aziz escorts her to the door of the whites-only club.

Summary: Chapter III

Inside the club, Mrs. Moore joins her traveling companion, a young Englishwoman named Adela Quested. They sit in the billiard room in order to avoid the performance of the play *Cousin Kate* that is taking place in the next room. Mrs. Moore has escorted Adela from England at Ronny's request; Adela and Ronny are presumably to become engaged. Mr. Turton, the collector of Chandrapore, enters and speaks highly of Ronny as the type of young man he likes.

The play lets out, and the billiard room begins to fill. Adela expresses her desire to see the "real India"—she wants something more than the stereotypical elephant ride most visitors get. Cyril Fielding, the principal of the local government college, passes through the room and suggests that Adela go see some Indians if she wants to see the "real India." The club ladies, however, are aghast at such a suggestion, and they inform Adela that Indians are creepy and untrustworthy. Nonetheless, Mr. Turton, eager to please Adela, promises to round up some Indians for a "Bridge Party" so Adela can meet some of them.

On the way home, Mrs. Moore points out the mosque to Ronny and Adela and speaks of the nice young man she met there. Ronny assumes from Mrs. Moore's tone that she is referring to an Englishman, and he becomes angry when he realizes she is speaking of an Indian. Back at the bungalow, after Adela goes to bed, Ronny quizzes his mother about her encounter. Using phrases he has picked up from his superiors, Ronny interprets each detail of Mrs. Moore's encounter as scheming on Aziz's part.

Ronny declares his intention to report Aziz to Major Callendar, but Mrs. Moore dissuades him. In turn, Ronny convinces his mother not to tell Adela about Dr. Aziz. Ronny worries that Adela will become too preoccupied with whether or not the English treat the Indians fairly. They finish talking, and Mrs. Moore goes to her bedroom. She notices a small wasp asleep on her coat hook, and croons to it kindly.

ANALYSIS: CHAPTERS I–III

Forster divides *A Passage to India* into three parts: "Mosque," "Cave," and "Temple." Each part opens with a prefatory chapter that describes meaningful or symbolic parts of the landscape. Chapter I of "Mosque" describes the city of Chandrapore and the surrounding area. The chapter begins and ends by mentioning the extraordinary Marabar Caves, yet the narrative reveals no detailed information about the caves. Instead, Forster portrays the caves as a symbol, the meaning of which is a deep mystery. The caves and their indefinable presence hover around the narrative from the start.

The description of the Indian city of Chandrapore and the English colonial buildings nearby suggests the wary and condescending attitude the British hold toward the Indians—an attitude the subsequent chapters examine in detail. The description of the English buildings, which lie some distance from the city and sit on higher ground, implies that the English intend to remain disconnected from the Indians and that they feel the need to monitor Indian activity. The narrator explains that Chandrapore appears misleadingly tropical and beautiful from the vantage point of the English buildings, and that newcomers must be taken down into the city to overcome their illusions about its beauty. Forster's description and commentary imply that the only two attitudes the English can have about India are romantic illusion or jaded disgust. On a broader level, his descriptions suggest the importance of all perspectives in the novel, the essential idea that what one sees depends on where—in both a physical and cultural sense—one stands.

The action of the novel opens in Chapter II with an argument between Indian friends about a topic that the novel explores in depth—the difficulty of friendship between an Englishman and an Indian. Though *A Passage to India* addresses the general political relationship between England and India, it approaches this issue on a personal, individual level. Mahmoud Ali and Hamidullah, rather than discuss the general issue of the subjection of India to British rule, focus on personal slights they themselves have suffered at the hands of individual English men and women. The conclusion the men reach after their argument reinforces this idea of connection and relation between personal and political matters: they conclude that an Indian can be friends with an Englishman only in England— implying that it is the structure of the colonial system that turns Englishmen disrespectful one at a time.

These tensions between the Indians and the English provide the main drama of the first few chapters. Forster generally portrays these interactions from the Indian point of view first—a perspective that invariably causes the incidents to reflect poorly on the English. At this point in the novel, the only offenses we see the English commit against the Indians are petty annoyances: Major Callendar interrupts Aziz's dinner with a summons and then disappears without leaving a note for the doctor, and then Mrs. Callendar and Mrs. Lesley completely ignore Aziz and steal his tonga. The dialogues at the club in Chapter III, however, hint at the darker, more damaging elements of the condescension of the English, as we see that English women, especially, can be snobbish and even cruelly racist.

Whereas the English appear rigid in their insensitivity toward Indians, the Indians seem to fluctuate in their feelings toward the English. Mahmoud Ali feels cynical and resentful at first, but he is also nostalgic and accommodating. Aziz, depending on his mood, reacts to the English with either bitterness or amusement. Hamidullah, too, remembers certain English people with real love, but he also sees many of them as tragically comic. Though the three Indian men sometimes stereotype to the same degree as the English, all three generally take a more thoughtful, complex view of their relations with the English than the English do.

SUMMARY & ANALYSIS

In addition to the broader sense of conflict between the Indians and the English, the opening chapters also focus on a tension surrounding the arrival of Adela Quested and Mrs. Moore in the city. Because the two women do not share their countrymen's sentiments about the Indians, they naturally conflict with the others at the club, and particularly with Ronny. Adela's remarks about her desire to see the "real India" prompt the club ladies to gather around her as though she were an amusing specimen or curiosity. Mrs. Moore, on the other hand, is quiet and introspective about her approach to Indian culture, arguing with Ronny about his viewpoints only when he draws her out. Even by this early point in the novel it appears that these tensions among Ronny's, Adela's, and Mrs. Moore's respective approaches to India and Indians may affect the question of Ronny and Adela's engagement, as well as Mrs. Moore's role in the engagement.

The encounter between Aziz and Mrs. Moore in the mosque stands out as the only successful interaction between an Indian and an English person in these opening chapters. The meeting is notable because Aziz and Mrs. Moore ultimately treat each other as equals and speak frankly as friends. Aziz recognizes in Mrs. Moore an ability to intuit rather than categorize, complimenting as "Oriental" her ability to sense whom she likes and dislikes without the help of labels. From this interaction comes the title of the first part of the novel, "Mosque." The correlation between the episode and the title suggests that Part I will focus on similar fleeting moments of friendship and attunement between the two cultures.

Beyond the verbal interaction that occurs between Aziz and Mrs. Moore, the encounter seems to include a religious or mystical undertone. The meeting takes place in a mosque, a place that is clearly holy to the Muslim Aziz, but also a place in which Mrs. Moore recognizes a clear divine presence. Before Mrs. Moore arrives, Aziz ponders the confluence of Islam and love in the structure of the mosque itself. Later, we see that Mrs. Moore recognizes that spirituality is based upon love for all other beings—hence her respect for even the tiny wasp sleeping in her room at the end of Chapter III. Mrs. Moore and Aziz appear drawn together not merely through good will, but through an inexplicable mystical affinity as well.

PART I, CHAPTERS IV–VI

SUMMARY: CHAPTER IV

Mr. Turton invites several Indian gentlemen to the proposed Bridge Party at the club. The Indians are surprised by the invitation. Mahmoud Ali suspects that the lieutenant general has ordered Turton to hold the party. The Nawab Bahadur, one of the most important Indian landowners in the area, announces that he appreciates the invitation and will attend. Some accuse the Nawab Bahadur of cheapening himself, but most Indians highly respect him and decide to attend also.

The narrator describes the room in which the Indian gentlemen meet. Outside remain the lowlier Indians who received no invitation. The narrator describes Mr. Grayford and Mr. Sorley, missionaries on the outskirts of the city. Mr. Sorley feels that all men go to heaven, but not lowly wasps, bacteria, or mud, because something must be excluded to leave enough for those who are included. Mr. Sorley's Hindu friends disagree, however, as they feel that God includes every living thing.

SUMMARY: CHAPTER V

At the Bridge Party, the Indian guests stand idly at one side of the tennis lawn while the English stand at the other. The clear segregation dismays Adela Quested and Mrs. Moore. Ronny and Mrs. Turton disdainfully discuss the Indians' clothing, which mixes Eastern and Western styles. Several Englishwomen arrive and discuss the earlier production of *Cousin Kate*. Mrs. Moore is surprised to note how intolerant and conventional Ronny's opinions have become.

Mr. Turton arrives, cynically noting to himself that each guest has come for a self-serving reason. Reluctantly, Mrs. Turton takes Adela and Mrs. Moore to visit a group of Indian ladies. Mrs. Turton addresses the Indian women in crude Urdu, and then asks Mrs. Moore and Adela if they are satisfied. One of the Indian women speaks, and Mrs. Turton is surprised to learn that the women know English. Mrs. Moore and Adela unsuccessfully try to draw the Indian women out into more substantial conversation. Mrs. Moore asks one of them, Mrs. Bhattacharya, if she and Adela can visit her at home. Mrs. Bhattacharya agrees to host the Englishwomen the upcoming Thursday, and her husband promises to send his carriage for them.

Mr. Fielding, who is also at the party, socializes freely with the Indians and even eats on the Indian side of the lawn. He is pleased to learn that Adela and Mrs. Moore have been friendly to the Indians. Fielding locates Adela and invites her and Mrs. Moore to tea. Adela complains about how rude the English are acting toward their guests, but Fielding suspects her complaints are intellectual, not emotional. Adela mentions Dr. Aziz, and Fielding promises to invite the doctor to tea as well.

That evening, Adela and Ronny dine with the McBrydes and Miss Derek. The dinner consists of standard English fare. During the meal, Adela begins to dread the prospect of a drab married life among the insensitive English. She fears she will never get to know the true spirit of India.

After Adela goes to bed, Ronny asks his mother about Adela. Mrs. Moore explains that Adela feels that the English are unpleasant to the Indians. Ronny is dismissive, explaining that the English are in India to keep the peace, not to be pleasant. Mrs. Moore disagrees, saying it *is* the duty of the English to be pleasant to Indians, as God demands love for all men. Mrs. Moore instantly regrets mentioning God; ever since she has arrived in India, her God has seemed less powerful than ever before.

SUMMARY: CHAPTER VI

The morning after Aziz's encounter with Mrs. Moore, Major Callendar scolds the doctor for failing to report promptly to his summons, and he does not ask for Aziz's side of the story.

Aziz and a colleague, Dr. Panna Lal, decide to attend the Bridge Party together. However, the party falls on the anniversary of Aziz's wife's death, so he decides not to attend. Aziz mourns his loving wife for part of the day and then borrows Hamidullah's pony to practice polo on the town green. An English soldier is also practicing polo, and he and Aziz play together briefly as comrades.

Dr. Lal, returning from the Bridge Party, runs into Aziz. Lal reports that Aziz's absence was noticed, and he insists on knowing why Aziz did not attend. Aziz, considering Lal ill mannered to ask such a question, reacts defiantly. By the time Aziz reaches home, though, he has begun to worry that the English will punish him for not attending. His mood improves when he opens Fielding's invitation to tea. Aziz is pleased that Fielding has politely ignored the fact that Aziz forgot to respond to an invitation to tea at Fielding's last month.

ANALYSIS: CHAPTERS IV–VI

The wildly unsuccessful Bridge Party stands as the clear focus of this portion of the novel. Though the event is meant to be a time of orchestrated interaction, a "bridge" between the two cultures, the only result is heightened suspicion on both sides. Indians such as Mahmoud Ali suspect that Turton is throwing the party not in good faith, but on orders from a superior. Turton himself suspects that the Indians attend only for self-serving reasons. The party remains segregated, with the English hosts regarding their guests as one large group that can be split down only into Indian "types," not into individuals.

Though the Bridge Party clearly furthers our idea that the English as a whole act condescendingly toward the Indians, Forster also uses the party to examine the minute differences among English attitudes. Mrs. Turton, for instance, represents the attitude of most Englishwomen in India: she is flatly bigoted and rude, regarding herself as superior to all Indians in seemingly every respect. The Englishmen at the party, however, appear less malicious in their attitudes. Mr. Turton and Ronny Heaslop are representative of this type: through their work they have come to know some Indians as individuals, and though somewhat condescending, they are far less overtly malicious than the Englishwomen.

Cyril Fielding, who made a brief appearance in Chapter III, appears here to be the model of successful interaction between the English and Indians. Unlike the other English, Fielding does not recognize racial distinctions between himself and the native population. Instead, he interacts with Indians on an individual-to-individual basis. Moreover, he senses that he has found like-minded souls in Adela Quested and Mrs. Moore. Of the two, Fielding is more closely akin to Mrs. Moore than Adela: Fielding and Mrs. Moore are unself-conscious in their friendship with Indians, whereas Adela consciously and actively seeks out this cross-cultural friendship as an interesting and enriching experience.

Forster fleshes out the character of Adela Quested significantly in these chapters. As part of this effort, the author uses Fielding as a sort of moral barometer, a character whose judgments we can trust. In this regard, we can see Fielding's judgment of Adela—that she appears to object to the English treatment of the Indians on an intellectual, rather than emotional level—as Forster's own judgment. Adela, perhaps because of this intellectual, unemotional curiosity about Indian culture, conducts her interactions in India in a negative sense rather than a positive one—attempting to *not* act like the other

English rather than attempting to actively identify with Indians. Adela always acts as an individual, rejecting the herd mentality of the other couples at the English club. While the other English try to re-create England in India through meals of sardines and plays like *Cousin Kate,* Adela hopes to experience the "real India," the "spirit" of India. Yet we sense that Adela's idea of this "real India" is vague and somewhat romanticized, especially when compared to Mrs. Moore's genuine interaction with Aziz or Fielding's enthusiastic willingness to partake in Indian culture.

The primary Indian protagonist, Aziz, develops in these chapters as significantly distinct from English expectations of Indian character. While the English pride themselves on dividing the Indian character into "types" with identifiable characteristics, Aziz appears to be a man of indefinable flux. Forster distinguishes Aziz's various guises—outcast, poet, medical student, religious worshiper—and his ability to slip easily among them without warning. Aziz's whims fluctuate in a way similar to his overall character. In Chapter VI we see Aziz shift from mood to mood in the space of minutes: first he wants to attend the Bridge Party, then he is disgusted with the party, then he despairingly mourns his dead wife, then he seeks companionship and exercise. Ironically, one of Aziz's only constant qualities is a characteristically *English* quality: an insistence upon good breeding and polite manners. This quality makes Aziz slightly prejudiced—it leads him to reject his friendship with Dr. Lal—yet it also allows him to disregard racial boundaries, as when he feels automatically affectionate toward Fielding because of the Englishman's politeness.

Furthermore, Forster uses these chapters to begin to develop one of the major ideas he explores in *A Passage to India*—the inclusiveness of the Hindu religion, especially as compared to Christianity. Forster portrays Hinduism as a religion that encompasses all, that sees God in everything, even the smallest bacterium. He specifically aligns Mrs. Moore with Hinduism in the earlier scene from Chapter III in which she treats a small wasp kindly. The image of the wasp reappears in Chapter IV as the wasp that the Hindus assume will be part of heaven—a point on which the Christian missionaries Mr. Grayford and Mr. Sorley disagree. Mrs. Moore is a Christian, but in Chapter VI we see that she has begun to call her Christianity into question during her stay in India. Whereas God earlier was the greatest thought in Mrs. Moore's head, now the woman appears to sense something beyond that thought, perhaps the more inclusive and all-encompassing worldview of Hinduism.

PART I, CHAPTERS VII–VIII

SUMMARY: CHAPTER VII

In every remark [Aziz] found a meaning, but not
always the true meaning, and his life though vivid was
largely a dream. (See QUOTATIONS, p. 75)

Fielding's many worldly experiences keep him from being insensitive toward Indians like the rest of the English are. The English mildly distrust Fielding, partly out of suspicion of his efforts to educate Indians as individuals. Fielding also makes offhand comments that distress the English, such as his remark that "whites" are actually "pinko-grey." Still, Fielding manages to remain friendly with the men at the English club while also socializing with Indians.

Aziz arrives at Fielding's for tea as Fielding is dressing. Though the two men have never met, they treat each other informally, which delights Aziz. Fielding breaks the collar stud for his shirt, but Aziz quickly removes his own and gives it to Fielding. The relations between the two men sour only briefly when Aziz misinterprets Fielding's dismissive comment about a new school of painting to be dismissive of Aziz himself.

Aziz is disappointed when Mrs. Moore and Adela arrive, as their presence upsets the intimacy of his conversation with Fielding. The party continues to be informal, though, even with the women present. Aziz feels comfortable addressing the women as he would address men, as Mrs. Moore is so elderly and Adela so plain looking.

The ladies are disappointed and confused because the Bhattacharyas never sent their carriage this morning as promised. Adela pronounces it a "mystery," but Mrs. Moore disagrees—mysteries she likes, but this is a "muddle." Fielding pronounces all India a muddle. Aziz denounces the rudeness of the Hindu Bhattacharyas and invites the women to his own house. To Aziz's horror, Adela takes his invitation literally and asks for his address. Aziz is ashamed of his shabby residence and distracts Adela with commentary on Indian architecture. Fielding knows that Aziz has some historical facts wrong, but Fielding does not correct Aziz as other Englishmen would have. At the moment Fielding recognizes "truth of mood" over truth of fact.

The last of Fielding's guests, the Hindu professor Godbole, arrives. Aziz asks Adela if she plans to settle in India, to which Adela spontaneously responds that she cannot. Adela then realizes that, in making this admission, she has essentially told strangers that she will not marry Ronny before she has even told Ronny so herself. Adela's words fluster Mrs. Moore. Fielding then takes Mrs. Moore on a tour of the college grounds.

Adela again mentions the prospect of visiting Aziz's house, but Aziz invites her to the Marabar Caves instead. Aziz attempts to describe the caves, but it becomes clear that Aziz has never seen them. Godbole has been to the caves, but he does not adequately describe why they are extraordinary; in fact, Aziz senses that Godbole is holding back information. Suddenly, Ronny arrives to take Adela and his mother to a polo match at the club. Ronny ignores the Indians. Aziz becomes excitable and overly intimate in reaction to Ronny's rude interruption. Fielding reappears, and Ronny privately scolds him for leaving Adela alone with Indians.

Before the ladies leave, Godbole sings an odd-sounding Hindu song in which the singer asks God to come to her, but God refuses.

> In her ignorance, [Adela] regarded [Aziz] as "India," and never surmised that his outlook was limited and his method inaccurate, and that no one is India.
> (See QUOTATIONS, p. 76)

SUMMARY: CHAPTER VIII

Driving away from Fielding's, Adela expresses annoyance at Ronny's rudeness. Adela mentions Aziz's invitation to the Marabar Caves, but Ronny immediately forbids the women to go. Ronny mentions Aziz's unpinned collar as an example of Indians' general inattention to detail. Mrs. Moore, tired of bickering, asks to be dropped off at home. Adela feels suddenly ashamed of telling those at the tea party of her intention to leave India.

After the polo match at the club, Adela quietly tells Ronny that she has decided not to marry him. Ronny is disappointed, but he agrees to remain friends with her. Adela sees a green bird and asks Ronny what type of bird it is. Ronny does not know, which confirms Adela's feeling that nothing in India is identifiable. Ronny and Adela begin to feel lonely and useless in their surroundings; they suddenly feel they share more similarities than differences.

The Nawab Bahadur happens by and offers Ronny and Adela a ride in his automobile. Riding in the back seat, the two feel dwarfed by the dark night and expansive landscape surrounding them. Their hands accidentally touch, and they feel an animalistic thrill. The car mysteriously breaks down on a road outside the city. They all climb out and determine that the car must have hit something, probably a hyena. After a short while, Miss Derek drives past them offers them a ride back to Chandrapore.

Driving back to Chandrapore, Miss Derek jokes about her employer, an Indian noblewoman. Ronny and Adela feel drawn together by their shared distaste for Miss Derek's crass manner and for the Nawab's polite but long-winded speeches. When Adela and Ronny arrive back at the bungalow, Adela says that she would like to marry Ronny after all. He agrees. Adela, however, immediately feels a sense of disappointment, believing she will now be labeled the same as all the other married Englishwomen in India. They go inside and tell Mrs. Moore of their plans. Adela begins to feel more pleasant, joining Ronny in poking fun at the Nawab Bahadur. When Ronny and Adela tell Mrs. Moore of the strange car accident, the older woman shivers and claims that the car must have hit a "ghost."

Meanwhile, down in the city of Chandrapore, the Nawab Bahadur describes the accident to others. He explains that it took place near the site where he ran over and killed a drunken man nine years ago. The Nawab Bahadur insists that the dead man caused the accident that occurred this evening. Aziz is skeptical, however, and feels that Indians should not be so superstitious.

ANALYSIS: CHAPTERS VII–VIII
Though Fielding himself disregards racial boundaries, his tea party does not quite develop into a successful version of the Bridge Party. Aziz and Adela both appear overexcited during the tea, while Mrs. Moore and Professor Godbole remain withdrawn from the others' chatter. The sudden cultural interaction carries Adela away and convinces her, almost subconsciously, that she cannot remain in India and become a wife at the club—prompting the spontaneous admission that upsets Mrs. Moore. The tea sours when Ronny arrives, though his rudeness appears only to bring out tensions that already existed. Aziz becomes grotesquely overfamiliar, Adela blames herself and Ronny, Fielding becomes annoyed, and Mrs. Moore becomes spiritually drained by Godbole's Hindu song.

The tea party is further disturbed by a disparity between what Forster calls "truth of fact" and "truth of mood." Thus far in *A Pas-*

sage to India, we have seen that the Indian characters often tend to say one thing when they mean another. Forster presents this tendency as problematic only for the English, among whom words are taken at face value. Indians appear skilled at identifying the undertones—the unspoken elements—of a conversation. Indeed, we see that Aziz recognizes from tone, rather than words, that Godbole is withholding information from his description of the Marabar Caves. Moreover, when Aziz invites Mrs. Moore and Adela to his house, the "mood" of his question—his sincere feeling of goodwill and hospitality to the Englishwomen—is all that Aziz means to convey. Adela, however, takes the invitation literally and asks for Aziz's address. The misunderstanding makes Aziz uncomfortable, as he is in fact embarrassed about the appearance of his home. Fielding, too, reacts negatively to Adela's literal-mindedness. This disconnect between cultural uses of language is an important division between the English and Indians in the novel.

Forster explores another divide between the English and Indian cultures through the idea of naming or labeling. If the English in the novel always say exactly what they mean, they also are quick to attach names or labels to objects and people around them. When Adela and Ronny sit together at the club, Adela wonders aloud what kind of bird sits on the tree above them. Ronny does not know, which depresses Adela even more; meanwhile, the narrator notes that nothing is identifiable in India, as things disappear or change before one can name them. The British in India realize that with the ability to name or label things comes power. It is for this reason that Fielding's remark that "whites" are really "pinko-grey" upsets the men at the club: by deflating labels like "white" and "brown," Fielding implicitly challenges the assertive naming and labeling power of the English in India. If "white" really only refers to skin tone—rather than also connoting superiority, advanced religion, technology, and morality—then "whites" have no inherent right to rule India.

Adela's conflicted view of naming or labeling constitutes a major tension within her character. On the one hand, Adela recognizes that the ability to label gives one power—or, as she might say, a purpose or place in the world. India's resistance to identification, symbolized by the nameless green bird, challenges Adela's sense of individuality. On the other hand, Adela realizes that being on the *receiving* end of a label can leave one powerless. It is for this reason that she remains resistant to marrying Ronny, knowing that she will be labeled an Englishwoman in India—a club wife—and that her behavior will be restricted accordingly. When Adela feels her individuality challenged by India's resistance to identification, she seems more likely to turn to Ronny for marriage; yet, when she recognizes the tyranny of labels like "Englishwoman in India," she feels reluctant to marry Ronny.

We see in these chapters that the natural environment of India has a direct effect on Ronny and Adela's engagement. As soon as Adela tells Ronny she does not want to become engaged, their surroundings begin to overwhelm them, making them feel like lonely, sensual beings who share more similarities than differences. In particular, they feel that the night sky swallows them during their ride with the Nawab Bahadur. The sky makes Ronny and Adela feel indistinct as individuals, suddenly part of a larger mass that is somehow fundamentally united. Therefore, when their hands touch accidentally in the car, both Ronny and Adela are attuned to the animalistic thrill of sensuality. Their experience under the engulfing Indian sky draws Ronny and Adela together, forcing them to assert themselves as important, distinct individuals through a commitment to each other.

Furthermore, the social environment of India—the Indians who surround Ronny and Adela—contributes to this shift in perspective in the couple's relationship, their new feeling that they are more alike than different. Specifically, Ronny and Adela feel a bond through their shared distaste for Miss Derek and the Nawab Bahadur—a bond that leads Adela to suddenly reverse her decision and renew her engagement to Ronny. In this regard, Forster implies that the union of marriage requires a third presence, against which husband and wife can define themselves as similar. Indeed, after announcing their renewed engagement, Adela shows her openness to her future with Ronny through her willingness to make fun of the Nawab Bahadur with him.

While Ronny and Adela feel a sense of unity against the muddle that is India, we see Mrs. Moore grow even more spiritually attuned to the minds of Indians. First Mrs. Moore appears to be most aligned with the religious figure of Professor Godbole. Godbole's song, in which God is called but does not come, profoundly affects Mrs. Moore, deepening her sense of separation from her Christian God. Then, when Ronny and Adela tell Mrs. Moore of their car accident with Nawab Bahadur, the elder woman strongly feels that a ghost caused the accident. Though Ronny and Adela ignore Mrs.

Moore, we learn a short while later that the Nawab Bahadur, too, suspects that a ghost caused the accident—the ghost of the drunken man that he ran over nine years ago near the same spot. While Ronny and Adela begin to segregate themselves from the social and natural landscape that surrounds them, Mrs. Moore surrenders to the overwhelming presence and mysticism she feels in India, attuning herself to a sort of collective psyche of the land she is visiting.

PART I, CHAPTERS IX–XI

SUMMARY: CHAPTER IX

Three days after the tea party, Aziz falls slightly ill. Exaggerating his illness, he remains in bed and contemplates a brief trip to a brothel in Calcutta to lift his spirits. Aziz takes a rather clinical view of his occasional need for women. Aziz knows that Major Callendar and others would be scandalized by his plans to visit the brothel. Nonetheless, Aziz does not mind breaking social codes—he simply tries not to get caught. Aziz suddenly notices that flies cover the inside of his room, so he summons his servant, Hassan, to dispose of them. Hassan is inattentive.

Hamidullah, Syed Mohammed, Haq, and Syed Mohammed's young nephew, Rafi, all crowd into Aziz's room to inquire about his health. Rafi gossips that Professor Godbole has also fallen ill. The visitors briefly toss around a suspicion that Mr. Fielding poisoned the men at his tea. Syed Mohammed and Haq discuss how all disease comes from Hindus. Aziz recites an irrelevant poem by an Urdu poet. Though not all of the men comprehend poetry, they are happily silent and for a moment feel that India is one. Hamidullah silently contemplates the nationalist meeting he must attend later in the day, which will gather Indians from many different sects. Hamidullah sadly considers that the group never achieves anything constructive and that the meetings are only peaceful when someone is denouncing the English.

The visitors announce their intent to leave, but they remain seated. Dr. Panna Lal arrives, under Major Callendar's orders, to check on Aziz. Dr. Lal immediately realizes that Aziz is not very ill, but he decides to cover for Aziz anyway, in hopes that Aziz will return the favor one day. After some prodding, Dr. Lal reluctantly reports that Professor Godbole's condition is not serious, which prompts the men to scold Rafi for spreading rumors. Dr. Lal's troublesome driver, Ram Chand, insults Rafi's uncle, Syed Mohammed, and a loud argument breaks out.

At this moment, Fielding walks into the room. Aziz would normally be humiliated at Fielding's seeing his poor, dirty home, but Aziz is distracted. Concerned about showing hospitality to Rafi, Aziz murmurs to the boy and tries to make him comfortable again after his scolding. Meanwhile, the men begin to question Fielding about his belief in God, the declining morality of the West, and what he thinks about England's position in India. Fielding enjoys being candid with the men. He explains that he is not certain that England is justified in holding India and that he is in India personally to hold a job. The men are shocked by the plainness of Fielding's honesty. Fielding, feeling disappointed by his first visit to Aziz, leads the other men out of Aziz's sickroom.

SUMMARY: CHAPTER X
Fielding and the others emerge from Aziz's home and feel oppressed by the weather and the general atmosphere outside. Several animals nearby make noises—the inarticulate animal world seems always more present in India than in England. The other men mount their carriages and go home, rather than back to work. All over India, people retreat inside as the hot season approaches.

SUMMARY: CHAPTER XI
Fielding stands on the porch of Aziz's house, but no servant brings his horse, for Aziz has secretly ordered the servants not to. Aziz calls Fielding back inside. Though Aziz self-pityingly draws Fielding's attention to the shabbiness of his home, Fielding is matter-of-fact in response. Aziz directs Fielding to a photograph that he keeps in a drawer, which is of his late wife. Flattered, Fielding thanks Aziz for the honor of seeing the picture. Aziz tells Fielding he likes him because he values men acting as brothers. They agree that the English government has tried to improve India through institutions, when it should have begun with friendship.

Fielding suddenly feels depressed, feeling that he cannot match Aziz's fervent emotions. Fielding wishes he had personal details to share with Aziz. Fielding momentarily feels as though he will not be intimate with anyone, but will travel through life, calm and isolated.

Aziz questions Fielding about his family, but the Englishman has none. Aziz playfully suggests that Fielding should marry Adela. Fielding replies vehemently that Adela is a "prig" who tries to learn about India as though it were a class at school. He adds that Adela has become engaged to Ronny Heaslop. Aziz is relieved, assuming that this means he will not have to host a trip to the Marabar Caves after all, as it would be unseemly to escort an engaged woman. Aziz agrees with Fielding's distaste for Adela, but Aziz objects to her lack of beauty rather than her attitude.

Aziz suddenly feels protective of Fielding and warns him to be less frank with other Indians. Aziz worries that Fielding might lose his job, but the Englishman reassures him that it wouldn't matter. Fielding explains that he believes in "traveling light," which is why he refuses to marry. Fielding leaves, and Aziz drifts off to sleep, dreaming happily.

ANALYSIS: CHAPTERS IX–XI

Though Forster clearly portrays the Indians in the novel more sympathetically than the British, he occasionally shows how the Indians sometimes succumb to racism in the same ways that the British do. Thus far, we have been acquainted only with Aziz and his similarly well educated, upper-class friends. In Chapter IX we meet several other acquaintances of Aziz, Muslims, some of whom are not as enlightened or privileged as Aziz himself. These men stir up an atmosphere of paranoia, suspicion, and racism equal to the behavior of the British: they first suspect Fielding of poisoning the non-English guests at his tea party, and then they blatantly disparage the Hindu religion. Forster satirizes their sentiments in the same way that he satirizes the British, showing how their racism leads them into contradiction. The Indians uphold the ill Hindu professor Godbole against the English Fielding, but then disparage Hindus in general as disease-ridden. The men, in their clamor about the alleged dirtiness of Hindus, resemble the English who fear infection or contamination from the Indians.

Similarly, though Forster satirizes English behavior toward Indians, he seems to remain somewhat pro-Empire in his views. Forster's logic does not argue against England's presence in India, but rather suggests that England might better serve India by improving personal relations with Indians. We can see Forster's fundamentally pro-Empire stance in his implication in these chapters that India, without British presence, would dissolve into fighting among its many sects. Hamidullah is Forster's mouthpiece for this sentiment in Chapter IX: as the other men disparage Hindus and bicker among themselves, Hamidullah contemplates the lack of national feeling in India. He notes that Indians from different sects—like those at his political meetings—unite only against the British. Forster portrays a united India as only a fleeting illusion, brought on by Aziz's recital of nostalgic poetry that imagines a single, Islamic India.

Furthermore, Forster implies that political action and energy may be impossible in India because the country is so oppressed by natural forces. In Chapter X, he shows that animals have as much voice as humans in India: their chaotic and meaningless noises sometimes dominate, blocking out rational human discussion. Additionally, the approaching onset of the hot season prevents action and sends people scurrying into the shelter of their homes. Looking closely, we see that each of the three parts of *A Passage to India* corresponds to one of the three seasons in India: Part I corresponds to the cold season, Part II to the hot season, and Part III to the wet season. As we see later, the oppressiveness of the hot season directly relates to the divisive and inflammatory plot events of Part II. Chapter X foreshadows the hot season and the turmoil, argumentativeness, and inexplicable sadness to come.

The majority of Part I has focused on developing the characters of Adela Quested and Mrs. Moore in relation to Aziz, to Ronny, and to their new surroundings. In these final sections of Part I, attention shifts somewhat to the character of Fielding, especially in terms of his relation to Aziz and to the rest of the English in Chandrapore. The development of Fielding's relations begins to constitute a second plotline throughout the rest of the novel, moving in parallel to plot developments involving Adela and Mrs. Moore.

Though Fielding is generally on friendly terms with the English in Chandrapore, Fielding's character presents a threat to the Englishmen because of his stance as an educator of individuals. The English fear that Indians become less obedient when they are better educated; indeed, the new ideas that Fielding fosters have the potential to undermine Britain's rule over India. The English see Fielding as suspect because his model of education works through interaction, sitting down with individuals and exchanging ideas. This model treats Indians as separate, distinct individuals, rather than a homogeneous and easily stereotyped group. As such, it places even Fielding himself—a representative Englishman—in a position of vulnerability. While other English people present themselves as knowledgeable and dominant, Fielding lets himself play the role of learner as well as teacher.

As Fielding grows apart from the Englishmen at the club, he grows closer to Aziz. In these chapters we see Forster set up these two characters as the potentially successful answer to the question of whether an Indian can ever be friends with an Englishman. More than merely a cross-cultural bridge, the friendship between Fielding and Aziz seems to develop a homosocial undertone as well. Aspects of heterosexual interaction dominate Chapter XI—the photograph of Aziz's wife, Aziz's happy thoughts of visiting prostitutes, the men's discussion of Adela's qualities—but these marks of heterosexuality function as a means to develop and cement a homosocial (but not implicitly homosexual) connection between Fielding and Aziz. These heterosexual tokens, conversations, and thoughts are passed between the two men and serve primarily to strengthen their relationship—though women are the focus of the men's conversation, women are effectively excluded, reduced to simply a medium of exchange between the men. Furthermore, we may interpret Fielding's sentiments against marriage in Chapter XI as Forster's own. The author implies that marriage shuts people off from educationally and emotionally fruitful relationships, such as the one that we see growing between Fielding and Aziz.

PART II, CHAPTERS XII–XIV

SUMMARY: CHAPTER XII
The hills containing the Marabar Caves are older than anything else on earth. The rocky hills thrust up abruptly from the soil and resemble nothing else in the surrounding landscape. Each cave has a narrow entrance tunnel that leads to a large, dark, circular chamber. If a match is lit inside the caves, its reflection appears clearly in the polished stone of the cave walls. The caves seem to embody nothingness; their reputation spreads not just by word of mouth, but seemingly through the earth itself or through the animals. On the highest hill of the rock formations precariously rests a large boulder, which is thought to be hollow. The hill is called Kawa Dol.

SUMMARY: CHAPTER XIII
Looking toward the Marabar Hills one day, Adela remarks that she would have liked to visit them with Aziz. Her servant overhears the remark, and exaggerated word of it travels to Aziz, who feels that he must make good on his earlier offer. The outing involves many

details and much expense on Aziz's part, but he organizes everything and invites Fielding and Godbole, along with the two ladies, to Marabar. Ronny gives permission for the women to go, as long as Fielding goes along with them.

The train that travels to the hills leaves just before dawn, so Aziz, Mohammed Latif, and many servants spend the night at the train station to avoid being late. Mrs. Moore, Adela, and the women's servant, Antony, arrive early in the morning. Adela dislikes Antony and, on Aziz's suggestion, orders him to go home. Antony refuses, however, on Ronny's orders, until Mohammed Latif bribes him to leave.

Though Fielding has not yet arrived with Godbole, Aziz is not nervous because he knows that Englishmen never miss trains. Aziz reviews the details of the trip with Mohammed Latif, who is to oversee the railway carriage. Suddenly, the train starts to move just as Fielding and Godbole arrive at the station. Fielding yells that Godbole's overlong prayers have made them late, and the Englishman tries unsuccessfully to jump on the train. Aziz becomes panicked and desperate, but Mrs. Moore and Adela reassure him that the outing will continue successfully without Fielding. Aziz suddenly feels love for the two women—Mrs. Moore especially—for their graciousness and blindness to race.

SUMMARY: CHAPTER XIV

> [Mrs. Moore] felt . . . that, though people are important,
> the relations between them are not, and that in
> particular too much fuss has been made over marriage.
> (See QUOTATIONS, p. 77)

Ever since they heard Godbole sing his Hindu song at Fielding's tea, Adela and Mrs. Moore have lived as though inside cocoons—not feeling anything. Mrs. Moore accepts her apathy, but Adela blames herself for her feelings of indifference. Adela even fakes excitement at times because she feels like she should be excited.

During the train ride, Adela thinks and chats with Mrs. Moore about her future plans. The elder Englishwoman, who is not in good health, feels impatient with marriage. She thinks to herself that society's valuation of marriage over other relationships has stunted its understanding of human nature.

Nearing the hills, the train comes to a stop next to an elephant. For Aziz's benefit, Adela and Mrs. Moore feign excitement about taking an elephant ride. Aziz feels happy and relieved, as he indeed went to great trouble to obtain the elephant for the outing. The group climbs up onto the elephant, and many villagers gather and walk with it to the Marabar Caves. In the pale early morning light, the landscape appears colorless and somewhat lifeless, suffused with an odd silence. Illusions abound, but there is no romance. Adela mistakes a tree branch for a snake; the villagers concur that it is a snake and refuse to let Adela correct their error. The group finally reaches the hills, but Adela and Mrs. Moore do not find them beautiful, and Aziz does not know enough about the area to act as an effective tour guide.

While Aziz's servants prepare tea for the women, Aziz reflects happily that the trip is a success thus far. He likens himself to the Mogul Emperor Babur, who never stopped showing hospitality and never betrayed a friend. The women ask Aziz about Babur and about another Mogul emperor, Akbar. Aziz has only contempt for Akbar, who foolishly thought he could use religion to unite all of India, when nothing can accomplish that goal. Adela expresses her hope that there will be something universal in India, if only to keep her from becoming snobby and rude like the other Englishwomen.

The group enters the first cave, which becomes crowded when the villagers follow them. Mrs. Moore feels crowded and she panics when something strikes her on the face. She is terrified by the cave's echo, which takes all sounds and reduces them to the sound "boum." The group exits the caves, and Mrs. Moore realizes that it was only a baby (from the retinue of servants accompanying the expedition) that hit her face. She politely refuses to enter another cave, but she encourages Adela to continue on with Aziz. At Mrs. Moore's suggestion, Aziz forbids the villagers to accompany them into the next set of caves.

Aziz, Adela, and the guide leave. Mrs. Moore tries to write a letter to her other children, Stella and Ralph, but she is haunted by the sound of the echo in the cave. The echo seems to suggest that nothing has value, and it renders even the words of Mrs. Moore's Christianity null. Mrs. Moore becomes despairing and completely apathetic.

ANALYSIS: CHAPTERS XII–XIV

Just as Part I begins with a chapter-long description of Chandrapore and its environs, Part II begins with a chapter-long description of the Marabar Hills and the caves. These descriptions set the tenor of the section to come; here, the narrative emphasizes the hills' alien quality of primitiveness and nothingness. The caves and the hills in which they are located predate all things known to humanity, including language and religion. The hills are described as "unspeakable"—an ambiguous term that not only connotes the hills' location outside time and human history, but also implies that they are a sort of desecration of the landscape. Indeed, the hills are distinctly nonhuman and seem to embody a physical nothingness. Forster uses the phrase "nothing, nothing" twice in the opening chapter, and we see that the word "nothing" recurs numerous times throughout Part II. This focus on absence, or lack, combined with the menacing, primal setting of the Marabar Hills, sets an appropriate tone for Part II, in which the personal relations built up in Part I fall apart. In Part II, individual characters become isolated, confused, and sensitive to an eternal force just outside their comprehension—a force of nothingness and emptiness that is embodied in the Marabar Caves.

Aziz's organized outing to the caves—the main event of these chapters and arguably of the novel as a whole—is fraught with misunderstandings and cruel ironies from the outset. A misunderstanding engenders the expedition to begin with: neither Aziz nor the women particularly want to go to the caves, but inaccurate currents of gossip convince Aziz that the ladies are eager to make the journey. Though Aziz plans the expedition meticulously, the entire affair is jeopardized, ironically, when Fielding—allegedly a stereotypically prompt Englishman—misses the train. Furthermore, though Adela and Mrs. Moore expect Aziz at least to provide them with an authentic view of India on the trip, they are disappointed to see that he has hired an elephant for them—a trademark of the inauthentic tours of India that the Turtons and other English colonials typically organize. Deepening the irony and misunderstanding, Aziz assumes that the women are delighted with the elephant, as he considers the animal a symbol of authentic India. Further irony comes from the fact that Aziz, who has never been to the Marabar Caves himself, is forced to act as the ladies' tour guide, because the only person knowledgeable about the caves—Godbole—has been left behind.

To add to the aura of misfortune hanging over the expedition, both Mrs. Moore and Adela are plagued by a spiritual or emotional deadness that they date to the moment when Professor Godbole sings his Hindu song in Chapter VII. Godbole's song resurfaces several more times in the novel, with the song's refrain—a supplication to God to "Come! come"—being especially important. In Chapter XII, Adela connects the refrain of the song to the Indian landscape, as she senses that the land appeals to someone, but offers nothing in return. Her concern with the countryside is also linked to her lack of excitement over the prospect of married life with Ronny in India. The refrain of Godbole's song, which assumes the presence of God but also asserts that God's presence will never be fulfilled, has awakened a lack of feeling in Mrs. Moore, and particularly in Adela. The women experience this emptiness and lack within themselves and also see it mirrored in the natural landscape surrounding them, which appears colorless and vacant.

Forster uses an interesting image to describe the emotional lack that Adela and Mrs. Moore feel, saying that the women have "lived more or less inside cocoons" since hearing Godbole's song. The image of the cocoon implies that the women are shut down, hibernating within themselves and cut off from others. Indeed, though Adela and Mrs. Moore maintain the pretense of polite interaction with Aziz, we sense that the two women feel disconnected from each other. Their conversation on the train is somewhat tense and awkward, and at one point Mrs. Moore even dozes off while Adela continues to speak. The image of a cocoon also suggests that the women are in a waiting period before a transformation or metamorphosis of some sort—a foreshadowing of the radical effect that the Marabar Caves soon has on each of them.

Forster also foreshadows the strange effect of the Marabar Caves through his depiction of the landscape leading up to the caves. He emphasizes the inorganic element of the setting: though living things exist within it, there is no color, no movement, and no vitality. Everything seems "cut off at its root," suggesting that the natural elements of the landscape have been perverted in some way. This perversion leads to a sense of illusion and confusion, as when Adela mistakes a stick for a snake. She corrects herself after looking through her field-glasses, but the villagers refuse to believe that the stick is not a snake after hearing her words. Within such a blank and empty landscape, words hold as much power as objects—and perhaps more. The natural world appears as a vacuum in which life does not exist, in which words fail to connect naturally to objects. Forster's descriptions of this unnatural, inorganic landscape prepare us for the Marabar Caves themselves, which seem to nullify vitality, incite illusions, and render Mrs. Moore and Adela unable to use language to describe their experience.

The horror Mrs. Moore experiences in the Marabar Caves is the most intense manifestation of the sense of emptiness that is at the core of *A Passage to India*. The strange nothingness of Mrs. Moore's experience is heightened by the fact that the episode is narrated not as it transpires, but in a more distant past tense than the immediate past tense that Forster uses in the rest of the novel. The effect is one of narrative absence, as if the narrator—and we as readers—must wait outside the cave, separated from the action until we learn of it through Mrs. Moore's recall. Initially, it is the darkness and closeness of the cave that alarms Mrs. Moore: it incites illusions, as when she mistakes a baby's hand for some "vile naked thing." But the most alarming and disturbing aspect of the cave for Mrs. Moore is its echo, which swallows all words and sounds uttered in the cave and returns them as "boum."

The echo is, in effect, a black hole in which difference and value are rendered nil and returned as a single repetitive syllable—"everything exists, nothing has value." The echo completely destroys the power of language and meaning, reducing everything from the smallest utterance to the loftiest ideas and pronouncements of the Bible—"from 'Let there be Light' to 'It is finished' "—to the same meaningless syllable. In short, the echo "rob[s] infinity and eternity of their vastness." This vision, in which good and evil are indistinguishable, is terrifying to Mrs. Moore. Thus far in the novel we have seen that Mrs. Moore embraces a rather mystical, holistic view of humankind as a single, unified whole. Here, however, she sees that unity—in the sense of sameness and indistinctness—can also be a terrifying thing, as destruction of difference in many ways entails destruction of meaning. For Mrs. Moore, this sudden realization renders her entire belief system meaningless, leaving her feeling stunned, flabbergasted, and powerless.

PART II, CHAPTERS XV–XIX

SUMMARY: CHAPTER XV

Aziz, Adela, and the guide climb up toward other caves higher in the
hills. Aziz's mind is preoccupied with breakfast preparations. Adela
is also distracted, as she suddenly realizes that she and Ronny are
not in love. Adela asks Aziz if he is married and if he has more than
one wife. The second question shocks Aziz, and he ducks into a cave
to recover. Adela follows shortly and enters another cave.

SUMMARY: CHAPTER XVI

Aziz exits the cave to find the guide alone. The two men hear the
sound of a motorcar. Aziz looks for Adela, and the guide explains
that she went into one of the caves. Aziz scolds the guide for not
keeping Adela in sight, and together they shout for her. In frustra-
tion, Aziz slaps the guide, who runs away. Then, with relief, Aziz
notices Adela already down the hills, speaking to a woman near the
motorcar. Aziz notices Adela's field-glasses lying broken on the
ground. He picks them up and proceeds back to camp, where he is
elated to find that Fielding has arrived in Miss Derek's car. Aziz
sends a retinue down to escort Miss Derek up to the camp, but Miss
Derek and Adela have already started to drive back to Chandrapore. Aziz cheerfully accepts this new development, but Fielding
senses that something is wrong with Adela.

Aziz, wanting to avoid the unpleasant memory of Adela's question about polygamy, has already refined the facts of their excursion
up the hill. Fielding presses Aziz for details because he feels the two
women have been rude to the Indian. Aziz, barely realizing he is lying,
reassures Fielding that the guide escorted Adela down to the car.

On the elephant ride back to the train, Fielding figures that the
expedition must have cost Aziz hundreds of rupees. The group
boards the train and rides back to Chandrapore. When they arrive
at the city, Mr. Haq, the inspector of police, boards the train and
arrests Aziz. Aziz panics and attempts to run out another door, but
Fielding stops him. Fielding calms Aziz, reassuring him that there
must be some mistake and that they will straighten it out together.
The two men walk out onto the platform, where Mr. Turton orders
Fielding to remain behind while Aziz goes to prison.

SUMMARY: CHAPTER XVII

Mr. Turton, looking fanatical and brave, informs Fielding that Adela has been "insulted"—presumably, sexually assaulted—in one of the Marabar Caves. Adela herself has lodged the complaint. Fielding protests that Aziz must be innocent. Turton informs Fielding that there is to be an informal meeting at the club that night to discuss the accusations. Turton explains that Adela is quite ill, and he is furious that Fielding is not as enraged as all the other English are. As Turton rides back to his bungalow, he looks with self-satisfied outrage at each Indian he passes.

SUMMARY: CHAPTER XVIII

Mr. McBryde, superintendent of police, receives Aziz politely at the jail. McBryde has a theory that Indians have criminal tendencies because of the climate—thus, the Indians' behavior is not their fault. Fielding arrives at McBryde's to get the details of the case. McBryde explains that Adela has claimed that Aziz followed her into a cave and made advances on her. She hit at him with her field-glasses and he broke the strap. McBryde shows Fielding the broken glasses, which the police have found on Aziz's person.

Fielding wants to ask Adela if she is completely sure Aziz attacked her. McBryde sends to Major Callendar for permission, but Callendar refuses because Adela is so ill. Mahmoud Ali and Hamidullah arrive in turn to consult Aziz.

Fielding continues to refuse to believe Aziz is guilty. McBryde begins to tell Fielding of a letter from a brothel owner that has been found in Aziz's house. Fielding does not want to hear details, however, and he admits that he himself visited brothels at Aziz's age. A police officer arrives with evidence from Aziz's bedroom, including pictures of women. Fielding explains that the photographs are of Aziz's wife. Fielding asks to visit with Aziz.

SUMMARY: CHAPTER XIX

Fielding runs into Hamidullah outside McBryde's office. While Fielding is anxious and impassioned, Hamidullah is calm and resigned. Hamidullah strategizes for Aziz's bail and defense team. Fielding feels deflated by Hamidullah's pragmatism and by the discrepancies in Aziz's story. But Fielding reassures Hamidullah that he is on "their" side, though he regrets taking sides at all.

Fielding returns to the college. Professor Godbole approaches Fielding about several trivial college matters. Fielding asks Godbole if he has heard about Aziz. Godbole has, but he quickly changes the subject. Fielding impatiently asks Godbole if he thinks Aziz is innocent or guilty. Godbole explains that according to his own philosophy, an evil action was performed at the caves, and that action was equally performed by Aziz, the guide, Fielding, Godbole himself, Godbole's students, even Adela herself. This response frustrates Fielding because it does not recognize the difference between good and evil. Godbole clarifies. Both good and evil are aspects of God, as God is present in good and absent in evil. Godbole then changes the subject again.

Fielding visits Aziz that afternoon, finding the doctor miserable and incoherent. Fielding leaves and writes a letter to Adela.

ANALYSIS: CHAPTERS XV–XIX

Aziz and Adela's hike to the higher caves is plagued by a sense of awkward sexual guilt and embarrassment. Aziz already feels somewhat repelled by Adela because of her lack of physical beauty and because of her upcoming marriage to Ronny, which will make her a rude Englishwoman like the rest. Meanwhile, Adela's startling realization that she and Ronny do not love each other makes her doubtful and ashamed. She unconsciously transfers her shame and discomfort to Aziz by insensitively asking him if he has more than one wife. Aziz resents this offense to his Western value system and ducks into a cave, feeling embarrassed both for himself and for Adela. Adela ducks into a different cave, feeling guilty about her lack of love for Ronny. While Aziz and Adela never meet in the same cave, Adela's mysterious experience of being "insulted" appears to stem from this prevailing atmosphere of sexual shame and embarrassment.

As with Mrs. Moore's experience in the cave in the previous section, Forster does not allow us to see Adela while she is actually in the cave, which leaves her attack a mystery to us. We do, however, see Aziz's thoughts and whereabouts during this time, so we know that he is innocent. As in the early parts of the novel, Forster gives us the Indian perspective first, upstaging the inevitably contradictory English viewpoint. Indeed, as we see in the upcoming chapters, the action continues to center on Aziz rather than Adela. While we see the English jump to conclusions about Aziz's guilt, we see Aziz inadvertently make himself appear guilty by trying to run from the police and by fudging his story to Fielding. Accordingly, Part II follows the plot of the wrongful incrimination of Aziz and its ramifications, rather than devolving into a routine mystery story about what really happened in the cave. Forster encourages us not to try to guess who or what might have attacked Adela, but rather to focus on the result—the racial tensions that erupt afterward.

Ironically, it is only Aziz who remains happy through the remainder of the Marabar outing. He is thrilled with the arrival of Fielding, and he does not let Adela's sudden departure bother him. The outing has affected everyone else negatively, however, and it has begun to divide them with accusations of blame. Mrs. Moore blames Miss Derek for Adela's hasty departure. Fielding blames Miss Derek and especially Adela for being rude to Aziz. Mrs. Moore and Fielding view each other as competitors for Aziz's affection. Finally, Fielding feels somewhat alienated from Aziz by what he sees as Aziz's impractical spending on an expedition for ungrateful Englishwomen. This sudden aura of blame and suspicion foreshadows the charges that are filed against Aziz, along with the broader tensions that those charges soon inflame.

The chapters immediately following Aziz's arrest are told from Fielding's point of view, which allows us to see how the alleged crime and arrest bring out the worst in both the English and the Indians. The English officials immediately and unreservedly assume that Aziz is guilty, and they go on to apply that guilt to Indians generally. Even the relatively reasonable Turton and McBryde are shocked and offended that Fielding would even think of standing up for Aziz. There is a tenor of self-satisfaction to the Englishmen's reaction, as though this crime confirms their long-held suspicions and stereotypes about Indians. The Indians, for their part, do not stand in defense of Aziz's moral character, but instead focus on details of evidence and legal process. As usual, Forster is more sympathetic in his portrayal of the Indian side, especially Hamidullah and Aziz's other friends, whose practical reaction to Aziz's arrest seems warranted by the clearly biased investigation. Still, both the English and Indians use the occasion of Aziz's arrest as a call to arms of sorts, an opportunity to consolidate sides and battle out racial tension that has long been simmering under the surface.

Though Fielding is reluctant to take sides in the uproar, the only person who stays completely aloof is Professor Godbole. When Fielding presses Godbole for his opinion about Aziz's innocence or guilt, Godbole offers only the philosophic musing that everyone is responsible for the evil action that has occurred at the Marabar Caves. Godbole's refusal to distinguish between good and evil recalls the all-equalizing, all-reducing echo that Mrs. Moore experiences in the caves. Yet while Mrs. Moore and Fielding both are unsettled by the muddle of good and evil, Godbole finds comfort in his philosophy, which concerns itself with eternal questions rather than minute particulars. Indeed, Godbole's Hindu viewpoint is not without a moral message. He implies that by meditating on the spiritual force that enfolds us all, we avoid the pitfalls of pointing fingers and assigning blame.

PART II, CHAPTERS XX–XXIII

SUMMARY: CHAPTER XX

The English gather at their club. The ladies feel compassion for Adela's suffering and suddenly regret that they were not nicer to her. As if to make amends, Mrs. Turton stands by the side of Mrs. Blakiston, a woman she previously snubbed. Mr. Turton calms the women, who fear for their safety.

Once the women leave, Turton speaks to the men. He tries to remain fair, though everyone else overreacts about the possibility that women and children are in danger. One of the men, a drunken soldier, recommends military presence, but Turton urges everyone to act normally. The soldier fondly mentions an honorable Indian with whom he played polo.

Major Callendar arrives to report that Adela is recovered. He sits with the soldier and tries to bait Fielding. Callendar gossips that Adela's servant was bribed to remain outside the caves, that Godbole, too, was bribed, and that Aziz ordered villagers to suffocate Mrs. Moore. Callendar loudly alludes to Fielding's alliance with Aziz, but Fielding refuses to be provoked. Callendar suggests that troops be called, but Turton is against using force.

Ronny arrives, and the men stand up and welcome him as a martyr. Fielding, however, remains seated. The drunken soldier calls attention to Fielding's rudeness. Turton confronts Fielding, who announces that Aziz is innocent. Fielding adds that he will resign from service in India if Aziz is found guilty, and that he resigns from the club effective immediately. Turton becomes furious, but Ronny tells him to let Fielding go.

Summary: Chapter XXI

Riding into Chandrapore, Fielding passes some children preparing for the celebration of Mohurram (an annual Muslim festival honoring the grandsons of the prophet Mohammed). Fielding meets with Aziz's friends, who have renewed Aziz's bail request and hired a famous anti-British lawyer from Calcutta.

Late that night, Fielding has the urge to speak with Godbole, but the professor is asleep. Godbole slips away to a new job a day or two later.

Summary: Chapter XXII

Adela, in shock, remains at the McBrydes'. Miss Derek and Mrs. McBryde treat Adela's sunburn and pick out the hundreds of cactus spines stuck in her skin from her run down the hill. Adela's emotions swing wildly. She sobs, then tries to logically review what happened—she entered, started the cave echo by scratching the wall with her fingernail, then saw a dark shadow move toward her. She hit at him with her field-glasses, he pulled her around the cave, then she escaped. She was never touched. Adela still hears the upsetting echo from the cave. She hopes Mrs. Moore will visit her and make her feel better.

When Adela's condition improves, Ronny retrieves her. McBryde and Ronny inform her that there was a near riot when the procession of the Mohurram festival attempted to enter the civil station. They explain to Adela that Das, Ronny's Indian assistant, will try her case. McBryde shows Adela a letter from Fielding, which has been opened. McBryde explains that Fielding has betrayed the English. Adela skims the letter and reads the line "Dr. Aziz is innocent."

Ronny takes Adela home. Adela is happy to be reunited with Mrs. Moore, but Mrs. Moore remains on the couch, withdrawn from Adela's advances. Adela tells Mrs. Moore about the echo she has been hearing, and Mrs. Moore responds knowingly. Adela asks Mrs. Moore what it is, but the older woman refuses to put it in words, and she predicts morbidly that Adela will hear it forever.

Mrs. Moore tells Ronny she will leave India sooner than planned. She will not testify at the trial. She will see her other two children into marriage, then retreat from the world. Mrs. Moore is sick of marriage—she sees little difference between love in a church and love in a cave.

Mrs. Moore leaves the room. Adela weeps, wondering aloud if she has made a mistake about Aziz. Adela thinks she heard Mrs.

Moore say, "Dr. Aziz never did it," but Ronny insists Mrs. Moore never said such words. Ronny finally convinces Adela that she is remembering lines from Fielding's letter. Ronny urges her not to wonder aloud if Aziz might be innocent.

Mrs. Moore returns, and Ronny asks her to confirm that she never said Aziz was innocent. Indeed, Mrs. Moore never made such a statement, but she nonetheless responds matter-of-factly that Aziz is innocent. Ronny asks for evidence. Mrs. Moore replies that Aziz's character is good. Adela wishes she could call off the trial, but she realizes how inconsiderate that would be to the men who have gone to so much trouble for her. Ronny decides to have his mother leave India as quickly as possible.

Summary: Chapter XXIII

The lieutenant-governor's wife offers to let Mrs. Moore travel back to England in her cabin, as all the other cabins are full. Ronny is relieved and excited that his name will be made familiar to the lieutenant-governor.

Though Mrs. Moore does desire to go home, she feels no joy, as she has passed into a state of spiritual apathy. She recognizes that there are eternal forces behind life, but she is indifferent to these forces ever since her experiences at the Marabar Caves. To Mrs. Moore, the echo in the cave seemed to be something very selfish, something that predated the world. Since that time, she has felt selfish herself—she even begrudges Adela all of the attention she has received.

Even so, Mrs. Moore's journey to Bombay is pleasant. She watches the sights outside her window and regrets she has not seen all that India has to offer. Bombay seems to mock her for thinking that the Marabar Caves were India—for there are a "hundred Indias."

Analysis: Chapters XX–XXIII

In the aftermath of Aziz's arrest, the English gather together in fear and solidarity. Using an ironic, satirical tone, Forster presents this abrupt shift of feeling as hypocritical. He shows how many of the English develop sudden compassion for people they previously snubbed, such as Mrs. Blakiston and Adela herself. Forster depicts this compassion as a momentarily genuine but generally self-serving, cathartic emotion. Perhaps the most perfect expression of the hypocrisy of this is the drunken English soldier's description of his polo partner as a model of the rare honorable Indian. In a twist of dramatic irony, the soldier does not realize what we know—that his polo partner was Aziz. This twist recalls the episode in Chapter VIII when Ronny remarks that Aziz's unpinned collar is emblematic of the Indians' general laziness; we know that the unpinned collar is actually a mark of generosity, as Aziz has lent Fielding his last collar stud to replace the Englishman's broken one. Forster frequently employs such dramatic irony in *A Passage to India* as an effective means of undermining English stereotypes of the Indians.

Many of the English take the assault on Adela as an assault by all Indians on the British Empire itself. Forster satirizes this overreaction as not only silly, but also dangerously based on sentimentality. Because of the presumed sexual nature of the assault, the English avoid speaking directly of the crime, the victim, or the perpetrator. The sense of mystery and sacredness that consequently surrounds Adela contributes to the Englishmen's understanding of this isolated incident as an attack on English womanhood itself. The Englishmen see English womanhood, in turn, as symbolizing the Empire and all that it stands for. The Englishmen therefore react frantically and disproportionately to the alleged crime, even going so far as to consider summoning an armed guard to police the whole Indian population.

The Englishmen's treatment of Fielding reveals the gap between Fielding's expansive worldview and the narrow-minded fear of difference that most of the English display. First, Fielding upsets the Englishmen's conception of the crime as unspeakable by mentioning both Adela and Aziz by name. Then Major Callendar and the soldier emerge as malicious and violent troublemakers who target Fielding because of his solidarity with the Indians—they imply that Fielding must choose sides, or else be treated as a spy or traitor. When Ronny enters the room and Fielding fails to stand up with the rest of the men, the others single-mindedly take Fielding's inaction as a slight to Ronny. Fielding alone sees both sides of the action, and he refuses to tacitly reject Aziz and India by standing. While the other men see the crime through the narrow, exaggerated lens of racism, Fielding implicitly endorses Godbole's universally-oriented philosophy that no action is isolated, that every action has many reactions.

When we finally hear Adela's side of the story about what happened in the cave, we learn that she did not make up the accusations out of malice. However, her memory sheds no additional light on the crime, as she is unable to put the experience into definitive language. Adela's naturally logical and practical mind struggles to convert the experience into narrative, but each effort breaks down, causing Adela herself to break down. Thus, we continue to see that the Marabar Caves seem to exert a primitive, powerful effect that upsets the power of language, meaning, and naming.

Much like Mrs. Moore, Adela is haunted by the constant presence of the echo from the Marabar Caves. Though Adela does not think about the echo in the same terms as Mrs. Moore, she appears similarly to have taken the echo as a malignant force. In the same way that Mrs. Moore feels the nullification of good and evil in the echo, Adela finds that the echo confuses moral distinctions. The echo causes Adela to oscillate between feeling like the victim of a crime and feeling like the perpetrator of an injustice who must beg forgiveness from all of India. Here again, the "boum" of the echo relates back to Godbole's philosophy—namely, the professor's conviction that all humans, including Adela herself, are responsible for the evil action for which Aziz has been arrested.

The differences between Mrs. Moore's response to the echo and Adela's response to the echo cement the differences between the two women as characters. Adela, who is practical and unspiritual, responds to the strange and confusing force of the echo by feeling more confident and certain of her status as a victim. Mrs. Moore, who is more attuned to eternal and intangible forces, is less resistant to the echo; she understands its force as negation. Yet while Godbole's Hindu philosophy maintains that absence and presence, nothing and everything, are one and the same, Mrs. Moore can only experience negation as a void. Overwhelmed by this emptiness, Mrs. Moore accepts her subsequent instinct that human actions matter very little. Consequently, unlike the other English, she does not become inflamed with indignance on Adela's behalf. Rather, Mrs. Moore treats the occasions of Ronny and Adela's wedding and the assault on Adela as essentially the same: love in a church is equal to love in a cave, she says. Yet while Mrs. Moore does not join everyone else in falsely condemning Aziz, she does not stand up for Aziz either—even though intuitively she knows him to be innocent. The echo, then, somewhat destroys Mrs. Moore's noble character, making her apathetic to the point of sickness and death.

With Mrs. Moore about to return to England and Adela suffering a breakdown, it seems that the two women's quest to understand India has been patently unsuccessful. On her voyage to the steamship, Mrs. Moore comes to understand the error she and Adela made. Whereas Mrs. Moore and Adela sought the "real India"—a romanticized essence—they should have understood that India is not so easily knowable, as it exists in hundreds of complex ways.

PART II, CHAPTERS XXIV–XXV

SUMMARY: CHAPTER XXIV

The hot season has begun, and everyone retreats indoors, away from the sun. The morning of Aziz's trial, the Turtons drive Adela to the courthouse with a police escort. On the way, Mr. Turton thinks to himself that he does not hate Indians, for to do so would be to denounce his own career and the energy spent on them. He concludes that it is Englishwomen who really make matters worse in India.

In front of the courthouse, students jeer at the car. Rafi, hiding behind a friend, yells that the English are cowards. Inside, the English gather in Ronny's office and loudly trade rumors about an Indian rebellion and Fielding's traitorous behavior. Ronny expresses confidence in his subordinate, Das, who is acting as judge for the case. Major Callendar loudly denounces all Indians. He relates with satisfaction that the Nawab Bahadur's grandson recently suffered severe facial injury from a car accident; all Indians should be similarly made to suffer. Everyone ignores Adela, who sits quietly, fearing she will have a breakdown during her examination.

When the case is called, the group files into the courtroom to their special chairs. Adela notices the lowly Indian servant operating the fan. He has a beautiful, godlike demeanor and appears aloof from everything taking place in the room.

McBryde opens the case for the prosecution. He presents as scientific fact his assertion that darker races lust after fairer races, but not vice versa. An Indian in the audience protests that Adela is ugly. Adela becomes flustered. Callendar requests that Adela be moved to the platform for better air. All of the English then move to the platform. Amritrao, the lawyer from Calcutta, protests that having all the English up on the platform will intimidate the witnesses. Das agrees that everyone but Adela must return to the floor. Outside the courtroom, word of this humiliation spreads, and the crowd jeers.

McBryde argues that Aziz lives a double life, simultaneously "respectable" and depraved. McBryde dwells on Aziz's attempt to crush Mrs. Moore in the first cave. Mahmoud Ali objects to this accusation, as Mrs. Moore will not be testifying at the trial. Mahmoud Ali bemoans the fact that Ronny has sent Mrs. Moore away, as she knew Aziz was innocent. Despite Das's attempts to restore calm, Mahmoud Ali shouts that the trial is a farce and all of them slaves. He leaves the courtroom in protest. The Indians begin chanting "Mrs. Moore" as if it were a charm, until the chant sounds like "Esmiss Esmoor."

Adela goes up to the witness stand. She suddenly feels like she is back at Marabar, and that it seems more lovely this time. As McBryde questions her, she visualizes each step of that day. When he asks if Aziz followed her into the cave, she requests a minute to answer. Visualizing the caves, she cannot picture him following her. She states quietly that she has made a mistake, that Aziz never followed her. The courtroom erupts. Callendar tries to halt the trial on medical grounds, but Adela confirms that she withdraws all the charges. The enraged Mrs. Turton screams insults at Adela. Das officially releases Aziz.

Summary: Chapter XXV

Adela is pushed along in the tide of Indians toward the exit. Fielding asks her where she is going. She responds listlessly, so he reluctantly takes her to his carriage for her safety. Fielding's students are gathered around the carriage. They convince Fielding and Adela to get inside and they then pull the two through town. Indians drape flowers around Adela, though some are critical of the two English sticking together.

The roads in Chandrapore are blocked with crowds, and the English are cut off on the way back to the civil station. Adela and Fielding are pulled back to the college. The phone lines are cut, and the servants gone. Fielding encourages Adela to rest and lies down himself.

Meanwhile, Aziz, in his victory procession, cries out for Fielding, who has abandoned him. Mahmoud Ali orders the procession to the hospital to rescue the Nawab Bahadur's grandson, as word has circulated that Mahmoud Ali overheard Callendar bragging about torturing the young man. The Nawab Bahadur urges restraint, but the crowd proceeds to the hospital.

Disaster is averted only by Panna Lal, who mistakenly believes the crowd has come to the hospital to punish him for offering to testify for the English. Lal acts the buffoon to honor the vengeful men, and he retrieves the Nawab Bahadur's grandson for them. The Nawab Bahadur averts further disaster by making a long-winded speech in which he renounces his loyalist title. He invites Aziz and friends to his house for a celebration that night. The baking heat of the hot season bears down on the city, and nearly everyone retreats indoors to sleep.

ANALYSIS: CHAPTERS XXIV–XXV

By the time of the trial, it becomes clear that the English value the sense of conflict that Adela's alleged assault has triggered much more than the welfare of Adela herself. The English solely focus on the vengeance to be had through Aziz's trial, ignoring the true trauma that Adela still suffers—the trauma of the echo. The less sympathetic English essentially ignore Adela, even on the morning of the trial, and instead engage in gossip about Fielding and inflated stories about Indian dissent and rebellion. Even the sympathetic, chivalrous Mr. Turton, who is attentive to Adela, thinks to himself that the general presence of Englishwomen in India is the cause of all English-Indian tension.

In the chapters that deal with Aziz's trial, we begin to see clearly the differences between Ronny's character and the character of the majority of the English. Though Ronny does not focus on Adela's personal pain more than any of the others, he does become somewhat more gracious in the aftermath of her ordeal. Adela's assault makes Ronny into a sort of martyr figure for the English, as his fiancée has been wronged; this status seems to release him from the English community's vengeance-seeking. During the trial, Ronny almost exclusively focuses on his subordinate, Mr. Das, who is trying the case. Ronny feels condescendingly confident in Das and looks forward to Das's successful performance as a good reflection on Ronny himself. Here, like Turton, Ronny is a character who feels confident in the British Empire and in the process of justice that the Empire brings to India. Though Ronny does not share the cross-culturally sympathetic character of his mother, Mrs. Moore, neither does he seek disproportionate revenge against the Indians, as many of the other English do.

The strategy of McBryde, the prosecution's lawyer, is to present his interpretation of the facts of the case in such a dry, emotionless, and "scientific" manner that they appear to be the truth. His interpretation of Aziz's actions and character resembles Ronny's interpretation of Aziz's meeting with Mrs. Moore in the mosque in Chapter III. Mrs. Moore acknowledged that Ronny's ungenerous interpretation, though it could be factually correct, ignored the warmth and trustworthiness of Aziz's character that she herself sensed. Here, McBryde's account similarly presents mere *interpretations* of fact as fact. McBryde's account is devoid of any recognition or sympathetic understanding of Aziz's honorable character. Additionally, McBryde's account—while presenting itself as "truth"—ignores specific angles of the case (such as the disappeared Marabar guide) and depends on biased character witnesses such as Panna Lal.

In response to the pretense of logic and fact that the English put forward, Mahmoud Ali emotionally argues that the English have conspired to withhold Mrs. Moore as a witness. This assertion prompts the Indian crowd in the courtroom to begin chanting Mrs. Moore's name. To the English, these actions are proof of the Indians' tendency to be overemotional and superstitious; Forster, however, presents the incantation of "Esmiss Esmoor" as a sort of collective Indian intuition about what is missing from the English pretense of justice. Mrs. Moore comes to symbolize an ideal, spiritual, sympathetic, and—perhaps most important—race-blind understanding. Though Mrs. Moore herself succumbs to apathy after her visit to Marabar and never offers to defend Aziz at his trial, she acquires an almost godlike significance through the rest of *A Passage to India*. Forster adeptly shows Mrs. Moore's shortcomings as human, yet also presents her as a positive symbol of unself-conscious and spiritually perceptive interracial understanding. Forster implies that Mrs. Moore's brand of extraordinary, undemonstrative compassion is what is missing from the English-style trial.

Adela is able to declare Aziz's innocence during the trial because she experiences a vision during her testimony. This vision is, in a sense, a positive version of the vision Mrs. Moore experienced after going into the first cave at Marabar. In that cave, Mrs. Moore has a vision of all differences being collapsed into the sameness of the echo, "boum." This lack of individuation and valuation frightens Mrs. Moore and makes her cease to care about individual relationships. Adela's vision is similarly impersonal. She experiences an out-of-body re-creation of her expedition into Marabar, and in it, she actually "sees" that Aziz did not enter the cave after her. The impersonal, detached point of view of this vision allows Adela to put honesty before her individual feelings or relationships with others. Forster foreshadows this revelation of Adela's relative unimportance when Adela first enters the courtroom and notices the poor but godlike Indian operating the fan. His aloofness and beauty suggest a detached, spiritual perspective from which Adela and her trauma appear less significant. Forster presents Adela's experience of spiritual impersonality as a positive vision that restores the balance of justice in the trial.

All the main events in *A Passage to India,* strangely, are actually nonevents. The event of Adela's experience of an assault in the Marabar Caves turns out to be an imagined assault. The event that should be Aziz's conviction is rendered a nonevent by Adela, who quietly affirms Aziz's innocence. Similarly, in the aftermath of the trial, the strain on English-Indian relations builds to a climax, but these tensions wither in the oppressive heat of the sun. The riotous Indians who gather at the Minto Hospital leave without violence to return home for naps. This anticlimactic tendency shows that Forster cares less about plot events than about how those events make an impression on individual characters and on the social atmosphere of the novel. Furthermore, the series of anticlimaxes reminds us of the pervasive sense of emptiness, absence, exclusion, and nothingness at the core of *A Passage to India*: more important than what we see occur is what we do not see occur; more important than what happens is what does not happen.

PART II, CHAPTERS XXVI–XXIX

SUMMARY: CHAPTER XXVI

Fielding reluctantly converses with Adela. She wants to discuss her behavior, but he is unwilling until she mentions that she has been ill. She says she has been ill with an echo since the day of the trip to the Marabar Caves, or perhaps the day she heard Godbole's song. Fielding admits that he always suspected she was ill, or perhaps hallucinatory. Adela cannot quite describe the vision she had in court. Nonetheless, Fielding appreciates Adela's meticulous honesty, and he apologizes for his rudeness to Ronny.

Adela asks Fielding what Aziz thinks of her. Fielding uncomfortably thinks about Aziz's contempt for Adela's ugliness. They discuss the possibility that the guide, or someone else, attacked Adela. Hamidullah arrives and is unhappy to see Fielding and Adela together. Hamidullah expresses severe disapproval of Adela because of the destruction she has carelessly brought upon Aziz. Hamidullah invites Fielding to the Nawab Bahadur's house for the victory celebration. Adela prepares to depart, but Fielding invites her to remain at the college while he stays with Aziz's friends.

Hamidullah, however, is eager to be rid of Adela, for her emotionless demeanor repels him.

While the two men discuss what to do with Adela, Hamidullah is relieved to notice Ronny pull up. Fielding meets Ronny outside and learns that Mrs. Moore has died on the voyage back to England and has been buried at sea. Fielding returns and sends Adela out. He and Hamidullah agree not to tell Aziz about Mrs. Moore until the next day. Adela returns, distraught at Mrs. Moore's death, and asks to remain at the college. At Fielding's request, Adela brings Ronny inside.

Hamidullah is unfriendly to Ronny. Fielding and Ronny settle the details of Adela's stay at the College, and then Fielding and Hamidullah leave for the Nawab Bahadur's celebration. On the way, Fielding overhears Hamidullah saying that Adela should be fined twenty thousand rupees. Fielding is distressed that Adela should lose her money and probably her fiancé as well.

SUMMARY: CHAPTER XXVII

> "Is emotion a sack of potatoes, so much the pound, to
> be measured out? Am I a machine?"
> (See QUOTATIONS, p. 78)

Late that night, the celebrants at the victory party are bedded down on the Nawab Bahadur's roof. Fielding and Aziz have a long talk. Aziz anticipates that Fielding will urge him not to make Adela pay any reparations. But Aziz no longer wants the English to admire him for his chivalry. Fielding explains that he himself changed his mind and now believes that Adela acted bravely and will suffer enough as it is. Aziz dismisses Adela because of her lack of beauty. Fielding becomes angry with Aziz's sexual snobbery.

Finally, Aziz says he will consult Mrs. Moore and do what she suggests. Fielding points out that Aziz's emotions are disproportionate: it was Adela who saved him, while Mrs. Moore went away—yet Aziz still loves Mrs. Moore and not Adela. Aziz rejects what he sees as Fielding's materialism, which measures love pound-by-pound. Fielding explains to Aziz that Mrs. Moore has died, but Hamidullah, overhearing their conversation, tells Aziz that Fielding is joking. Aziz takes it as a joke.

Summary: Chapter XXVIII

In Chandrapore, a legend arises that Ronny killed his mother for attempting to save Aziz's life. Two different tombs are reported to contain Mrs. Moore's body, and townspeople leave offerings at both tombs.

The English do not respond to the rumors. Ronny knows that he was inconsiderate to his mother at the end, but he blames her for the trouble she continues to make with the legend of her death. Ronny hopes that troublesome Adela will leave India, too. He has not yet broken off their engagement, hoping that she will realize the marriage would ruin his career, and therefore back out politely.

Summary: Chapter XXIX

> *Perhaps life is a mystery, not a muddle. . . . Perhaps*
> *the hundred Indias which fuss and squabble so*
> *tiresomely are one, and the universe they mirror is*
> *one.* (See QUOTATIONS, p. 79)

The lieutenant-governor arrives in Chandrapore to survey the aftermath of the Marabar case. He congratulates Fielding for his upstanding behavior before and during the trial. Adela continues to stay at the college, and she and Fielding talk more frequently. He helps her draft an apology to Aziz. The apology seems unsatisfactory: though Adela is just, she does not truly love India and Indians.

Aziz and Fielding begin to quarrel about future plans and about Adela's reparation payment. Fielding resorts to a mention of Mrs. Moore, and finally Aziz gives in and agrees to ask Adela only to repay his legal costs. As Aziz has predicted, his generosity wins him no prestige among the English, who will believe forever that he committed the crime.

Ronny visits Adela at the college and breaks off their engagement. Adela and Fielding talk afterward. Adela sadly repents for all the trouble she has caused everyone. She admits, though, that she and Ronny should not have thought about marriage in the first place. Like old friends, Fielding and Adela talk about the difficulties of love. Fielding questions Adela about the incident in the cave one final time. Indifferently, she accepts that it was the guide who assaulted her. She explains that only Mrs. Moore knew for sure, perhaps by telepathy. Fielding and Adela continue to chat, but their practicality and friendliness are slightly plagued by a sense of something indefinable and infinite in the universe.

Adela takes a ship home to England. She decides on the way to look up Mrs. Moore's two other children, Ralph and Stella, when she arrives.

ANALYSIS: CHAPTERS XXVI–XXIX

In Fielding and Adela's conversations after the trial, Forster focuses not on conjecture about what might have happened to Adela in the cave, but rather on the uneasiness of two unspiritual people with a mysterious and otherworldly event. Fielding and Adela's discussions of Marabar and Adela's testimony at the trial raise ideas of ghosts and visions with which both are uncomfortable. The two begin to sense that "life is a mystery, not a muddle," in Forster's words. To fend off these uncomfortable ideas, the two find solace in scientific words like "hallucination," or in the possibility that another culprit, such as Aziz's guide, was responsible for a real, physical attack. Forster presents the conversations between Fielding and Adela as fluctuations between a spiritual recognition of something infinite and eternal and a comforting return to the familiarity of traditional English rationalism.

The announcement of Mrs. Moore's death further troubles this sense of English rationalism, particularly for Adela. Adela is struck by the realization that Mrs. Moore died at just about the time when the Indians in the courtroom crowd began chanting her name. This simultaneity further associates Mrs. Moore with mystical power and suggests that her spirit is present in the courtroom—a sense that Aziz confirms. Additionally, the fact that Mrs. Moore is buried at sea further implies that she is not of either world, India or England, but permanently occupies a liminal space between them. Though Forster presents the cult of Mrs. Moore that emerges in Chandrapore as silly and superstitious, he nevertheless implies that the woman's spirit represents significant mystical power.

Though Adela bravely resists the encouragement of the English contingent when she pronounces Aziz innocent, Aziz, Hamidullah, and many other Indians continue to hold a grudge against her—a grudge that reinforces a dichotomy between Indian values and English values. The Indians hold a grudge not because of Adela's responsibility for Aziz's downfall, but because her rescue of Aziz is so emotionless. The Indians sense no kindness or love behind Adela's action, so they suspect it is an insincere trick. Again, Forster sets up a dichotomy between the English focus on literal honesty and the Indian focus on the emotions lying behind actions or words. The Indians' resistance to Adela mirrors their resistance to the British Empire as a whole, which similarly administers justice without sincere compassion or kindness.

Though Forster's critique of the British Empire has hitherto been the same critique the Indians themselves make—that the Empire lacks imaginative compassion—his critique begins to shift after Adela's trial. Fielding, who generally serves as the mouthpiece for Forster in the novel, begins to feel wary of the Indian attention to imaginative compassion over all else. Fielding believes that Aziz's preoccupation with kindness blinds him to the fact that Adela has taken more action on his behalf than Mrs. Moore ever did. Aziz resents the implication that his emotions should be perfectly measured, as he feels that this view does not account for his nonliteral, nonlinguistic idea of love. Fielding, however, increasingly suspects that imagination betrays those who depend on it to the exclusion of all else. If Forster has shown in Part I of *A Passage to India* that most English suffer from a lack of imagination and compassion, he shows toward the end of Part II that too much imagination and compassion has the potential to lead the Indians astray.

Perhaps the clearest example of imagination leading Indians astray in these chapters is the initial rift between Fielding and Aziz. When Fielding accompanies Adela back to the college directly after the trial, Aziz feels that Fielding has abandoned him. We know, however, that Fielding has perfectly good reason to fear for Adela's safety, and that he has no intention whatsoever of neglecting Aziz. Aziz gets carried away in his somewhat self-pitying sense of Fielding's betrayal, and the relationship between the two men begins to break apart.

Fielding, for his part, becomes increasingly disillusioned with his Indian friends in general. He feels that Aziz, Hamidullah, and others are unnecessarily cruel in seeking incredible sums of monetary compensation from Adela. Fielding is also surprised by Hamidullah's nastiness to both Adela and Ronny. Indeed, in these chapters, Forster's satire on English behavior gives way somewhat to a sense of disappointment with Indian behavior. The Indians, in reaction to their victory at the trial, become aggressive, start to complain of new, nonexistent mistreatments, and even resort to petty lawlessness. The English virtually vanish from the novel, as Forster's critique—though never satiric—turns toward the Indians instead.

PART II, CHAPTERS XXX–XXXII

SUMMARY: CHAPTER XXX

One consequence of Aziz's trial is improved relations between Hindus and Muslims in Chandrapore. Mr. Das visits Aziz one day at the hospital and asks Aziz to write a poem for his magazine. The magazine readership is mostly Hindu, but Das hopes to make it appeal to the general Indian and believes that Aziz's poem might help. Aziz agrees and goes home to write. All his attempts at poetry are too extreme, though—they veer toward too-sad pathos or too-harsh satire. Aziz tries to envision a successful poem for Das, and this speculation leads him to visions of a successful India. Aziz vows to be friendly to Hindus and to hate the British. His character becomes hardened.

Aziz meets with Hamidullah one day and explains his plan to take a job in a Hindu state. Hamidullah protests that such a job will not pay enough and scolds Aziz again for not making Adela pay reparations. Then Hamidullah passes on a rumor he has heard that Fielding was having an affair with Adela during her stay at the college. Aziz becomes explosive, yelling that everyone has betrayed him.

When Aziz calms down, he and Hamidullah prepare to visit the women of Hamidullah's household in purdah. Hamidullah mentions that the women seemed to be ready to give up purdah at the time of Aziz's trial, but that they have not yet done so. Hamidullah suggests that Aziz take a realistic view of the Indian lady as a subject for a poem.

SUMMARY: CHAPTER XXXI

Aziz muses on the rumor of Adela and Fielding for several days, eventually believing it to be fact. When Fielding returns from a conference, Aziz picks him up and tries to address the rumor indirectly, mentioning that McBryde and Miss Derek were caught having an affair. Fielding is uninterested in this gossip, however. Finally, Aziz overtly mentions the rumor about Adela and Fielding, expressing fear that the affair will hurt Fielding's reputation. Aziz clearly is fishing for a straightforward denial, but Fielding does not provide one. Instead, Fielding chides Aziz for worrying too much about reputation and propriety. Aziz finally takes it for granted that Fielding and Adela were having an affair, and he states this directly. Fielding, startled, blows up at Aziz. Aziz is immediately pained at his own mistake and Fielding's harsh words. Aziz agrees, reluctantly, to have dinner with Fielding that night.

Fielding runs into Turton at the post office. Turton demands Fielding's presence at the Englishmen's club at six that evening. Fielding stops by the club briefly to find that many new officials have replaced the old ones, but the tenor feels the same. Fielding likens this repetitive bigotry to an evil echo.

At dinner, Fielding tells Aziz that he is traveling to England briefly on official business. Aziz changes the subject to poetry. Fielding expresses hope that Aziz will be a religious poet, because though Fielding is an atheist, he thinks there is something important in religion that has not yet been celebrated—perhaps something in Hinduism. Aziz asks if Fielding will visit Adela in England. Fielding indifferently says that he probably will. At this, Aziz rises to leave. Fielding asks forgiveness for his harshness that morning, but Aziz rides away feeling depressed. He suspects that Fielding is going to England to marry Adela for her money. Aziz decides to travel with his children tomorrow, so that Fielding will be gone for England by the time he returns.

SUMMARY: CHAPTER XXXII
Fielding's ship journeys up to the Mediterranean and then docks at Venice. With a feeling of disloyalty, Fielding rediscovers his appreciation for form in architecture. Unlike the random temples and lumpy hills of India, the Venetian buildings appear in harmony with the earth. Fielding feels divided from his Indian friends because of their inability to appreciate form that has "escaped muddle." On arriving in springtime England, Fielding feels a romantic sense reawakening in him.

ANALYSIS: CHAPTERS XXX–XXXII
A Passage to India might have ended after Aziz's trial, but it continues for many more chapters, as Forster clears the ground for the new concerns of the novel. Many elements of the pre-trial community of Chandrapore break up in the aftermath of the trial. Some of the English officials, such as Ronny Heaslop and Major Callendar, are assigned to new posts in distant cities. Ronny and Adela break their engagement, and Adela returns to England. Mrs. Moore leaves for England and dies. Godbole takes a new position in a distant state.

Finally, the two main characters who remain—Aziz and Fielding—undergo serious changes, of both setting and character.

Though Forster presents Adela as brave and well intentioned in testifying to Aziz's innocence, the author by no means allows us to forget the negative consequences of her initial accusation. Aziz's arrest reveals to Indians the deep hatred that the majority of English feel for them at all times. Aziz's time in prison hardens him generally about personal relationships and teaches him to be cynical about the English in particular. Whereas the Aziz of the early parts of the novel is open to friendship with anyone, regardless of race, his openness is now prejudiced by his universal hatred for the English. Aziz feels less and less that friendship has the power to overcome cultural or racial differences.

The single positive effect of the trial is that the Hindu and Muslim communities in Chandrapore begin to come together and overcome their existing animosity. Heartened by these advances, Aziz makes a conscious effort to turn his mind toward a vision of a motherland. Uncharacteristically, he remains steadily focused on the goal of an independent India. He turns his poetry away from nostalgic invocations of Islam and toward a realistic suggestion of what India really is and could be. In these later chapters, then, Forster comes across as less invested in the idea that the British Empire is the best way to rule India. Through Aziz's musings we get a prescient sense of a multicultural, independent India—an India that, in reality, finally formed twenty-five years after the publication of Forster's novel.

These later chapters of the novel shift concern from the broader picture of English-Indian relations to a smaller focus on the breakup of Aziz and Fielding's friendship. Even after the divisive Adela leaves India, Aziz and Fielding continue to grow apart. Aziz's characteristic overactive imagination and distrust of evidence and reason continue to plague him when the rumor of Adela and Fielding's affair reaches him. Even Fielding's denial of the rumor does not dispel Aziz's suspicion, as he already feels Fielding drifting away from him and becoming less trustworthy. Aziz's Indian friends encourage him in his suspicions, as they include Fielding in their backlash against the English after the trial. Fielding, for his part, is gradually drawn—though perhaps unwillingly—back into the English circle, especially after the lieutenant-governor approves of Fielding's actions during the trial.

Sexuality continues to remain a significant and constant barrier to the connection between Aziz and Fielding. When the two men discuss the rumored affair with Adela, Fielding is so shocked that Aziz believed the rumor that he calls Aziz a "little rotter" and immediately regrets it. Forster attributes the tense misunderstanding between the two men to the tension that arises when two people do not think of sex in the same way. Sex has always been a point of contention for the two men because Fielding resents Aziz's crass attitude toward female beauty and sexuality. In the same way that sex troubles Aziz and Fielding, Adela's painful thoughts about sexuality and her impending marriage to Ronny may be what cause her to imagine an assault in the Marabar Caves. Sexuality in *A Passage to India* is never a connecting force between characters, but rather a divisive one that sends the characters back into their shells.

In one of the only genuine and unstrained moments of their conversation over dinner in Chapter XXXII, Aziz and Fielding each foreshadow the events and concerns of Part III of the novel. Fielding, though an atheist, senses something in the Hindu religion that could be valuable, that is still "unsung." Aziz then has a brief vision of himself living in a "Hindu jungle Native State." As we soon see, Part III, which takes place two years later, features Aziz in a new position in Mau, just such a Hindu Indian-ruled jungle state. Indeed, Part III takes Hinduism as its backdrop, suggesting just what Fielding has implied—that in Hinduism may lie the mysterious remedy to cultural and individual conflict.

Fielding's brief stop in Italy on the way to England, especially his admiration of Venetian architecture, continues Forster's exploration of architecture as representative of the cultural differences between East and West. The Western architecture of Venice shows the triumph and beauty of logical form. Building and earth complement each other, and proportions relate correctly. In Forster's eyes, Western architecture signifies everything that is positive about the logic, literalness, and reason of the West and Western thought. Fielding is uneasy about his appreciation of Venice because he knows that such appreciation—like the Englishmen's salute of the tragic Ronny in Chapter XX—implicitly rejects India. From Fielding's point of view, the worst, most "muddled" qualities of India are represented in its architecture, which to him is disproportionate, unpredictable, and formless.

PART III, CHAPTERS XXXIII–XXXV

SUMMARY: CHAPTER XXXIII

Two years later, and hundreds of miles west of Chandrapore, Aziz lives and works as physician to the Rajah in the Indian-ruled, Hindu city of Mau. Professor Godbole also works there as minister of education.

That night at the royal palace, the Hindus of Mau celebrate the midnight birth of the god Krishna. Professor Godbole leads his small choir in singing hymns. On the wall, one of many multilingual signs proclaims "God si love" rather than "God is love." The crowd is large, but calm. Confusion abounds, but the celebrants wear expressions of joy that make them all seem alike. The singers seem to become one with the universe and to love all men. Godbole straightens his pince-nez and thinks momentarily of Mrs. Moore, and then of a wasp he once saw sitting on a stone. Godbole tries to incorporate the stone, along with Mrs. Moore and the wasp, into his vision of the oneness of the universe, but his conscious effort fails.

As midnight approaches, Godbole and the rest of the crowd begin to dance and shout. The aging and sick Rajah, the ruler of the state, arrives to witness the birth ceremony. At midnight, the crowd heralds the birth of Krishna, the embodiment of Infinite Love. After overseeing the birth with tears of joy, the Rajah is taken away to see Aziz, who tends to him. The crowd continues to celebrate for Krishna's benefit with practical jokes, confused frolic, and playful games.

SUMMARY: CHAPTER XXXIV

On the way to his house, Aziz runs into Godbole on the street. Godbole, still in religious ecstasy, manages to tell Aziz that Fielding has arrived at the European guest house. Fielding has come to Mau on official business, to check on education.

Aziz reflects happily on Godbole, who got Aziz his position at Mau. Aziz is pleased with Mau, where rivalries exist only between Hindu Brahmans and non-Brahmans, not Muslims or Englishmen. Though Aziz is a Muslim himself, the Hindu people of Mau accept him because he is respectful.

Aziz does not want to see Fielding. He ceased to communicate with Fielding after reading half of a letter from Fielding in England that seemed to say Fielding had married Adela Quested. Aziz finally feels like a true Indian through his hatred of the English, and he is happy with his life away from English-ruled India. His children live with him and he writes poetry. Aziz's poetry addresses the need to abolish the purdah and to create a new motherland. His life is only mildly disrupted by the local English political agent, Colonel Maggs, who has orders to watch Aziz as a suspected criminal.

Arriving home, Aziz finds a formal note from Fielding, forwarded from Godbole, announcing the arrival of himself, his wife, and his brother-in-law. The note, like all notes from visiting Englishmen, asks for specific amenities and advice. Aziz tears up the note.

Summary: Chapter XXXV

In Aziz's garden lies part of a shrine in honor of a young Muslim saint who once freed all the prisoners in the local fort before the police beheaded him. Aziz has come to associate the saint with his own time in prison, and to appreciate the shrine.

The morning after receiving Fielding's note, Aziz walks with his children to the other section of the shrine, which lies a short distance from their house. Aziz and the children wander through the small shrine and adjoining mosque, and then admire the view from the old fort. It is the rainy season and the water tanks are full, promising a good crop to come.

A line of prisoners walks nearby. The children ask the prisoners which of them will be freed that night during the traditional Hindu procession of the Chief God. The Chief God moves through town, stops at the jail, and pardons one prisoner. The low-caste prisoners politely discuss the matter with Aziz's family. The prison guard asks Aziz about the Rajah's health. Aziz says that the Rajah's condition has been improving, though in reality the Rajah died the night before. Aziz is to keep the Rajah's death a secret until the festivities end.

Aziz's children notice that Fielding and his brother-in-law are climbing up the ridge to the shrine. The two men enter the shrine, but a swarm of bees chases them out. Fielding's brother-in-law is stung, and Aziz walks over to attend to the wound. Fielding, in an unfriendly tone of voice, asks Aziz why he never responded to any of his letters. Suddenly, heavy rain begins to fall, and they hurry down to the road to Fielding's carriage.

Aziz helps the others into the carriage, referring to Fielding's brother-in-law as "Mr. Quested." Fielding is shocked, for he married Mrs. Moore's daughter, Stella, not Adela Quested—thus the brother-in-law is Mr. Moore. Aziz is suddenly embarrassed and elated. Fielding realizes the mistake that has caused Aziz's unfriendliness. With little sympathy, Fielding blames the mix-up on Mahmoud Ali, who knew that Fielding married Stella. Fielding explains that Mahmoud Ali even referred to her as "Heaslop's sister" in a letter. The name Heaslop infuriates Aziz, who is already angry at the realization of his mistake.

Aziz asks Fielding not to visit him while in Mau. Aziz explains that he still feels almost as betrayed as if Fielding had actually married his enemy and taken what should have been his reparation money. On the other hand, Aziz forgives Mahmoud Ali all things because Mahmoud Ali loved him. Aziz gathers his children around him and states in Urdu that he wishes no Englishman or Englishwoman to be his friend. Aziz returns home feeling excited.

ANALYSIS: CHAPTERS XXXIII–XXXV

Part III, like Parts I and II, begins with an introductory chapter that sets the tone of the section. This time, Forster describes in detail the Hindu celebration of Krishna's birth at the royal palace at Mau. The celebration is disorderly, mirroring the "muddle" of India itself throughout of the novel: multiple musicians play different songs, not enough seats are available, and a sign on the wall confusingly proclaims, "God si Love." Yet the mystical traditions of the ceremony transform the muddle into mystery. The overlarge crowd is strangely calm and happy, as each person surrenders himself into the moment. The Hindu celebration, which provides the backdrop for all of Part III, offers a vision of individualism merged into a complete collectivity—a dynamic in which all living things are one with love and no hierarchies exist.

During the birth ceremony, Godbole thinks briefly of Mrs. Moore and a wasp. The wasp, which appears throughout *A Passage to India,* represents the fact that even the lowliest creatures are still incorporated into the Hindu vision of the oneness of the universe. The wasp in Chapter XXXIII recalls Mrs. Moore's gentle appreciation of the wasp in her bedroom on the night she meets Aziz in the mosque in Chapter III. Mrs. Moore's contemplation of the wasp suggests that she was open to the collectivity of Hinduism. Likewise, Godbole's vision of Mrs. Moore and the wasp, suggests that the professor, as a Hindu, has sensed the Englishwoman's sympathy with

Hinduism. Indeed, the vision of the mystical Mrs. Moore, along with Godbole and the Hindu religion, serves as a backdrop for Part III of the novel.

In the two years that have passed between the end of Part II and the beginning of Part III, Aziz and Fielding's relationship has completely fallen apart. Aziz appears mostly at fault for this quarrel, as he has mistakenly assumed that Fielding married Adela Quested, failing to take the time to check the truth of his assumption. Impetuously, Aziz has completely shut himself off from Fielding. Forster implies that Aziz's overactive imagination and suspicion—though they once served him well—have gotten the better of him, as he has relied upon them too much. Fielding, meanwhile, appears to have become the stereotypical Englishman in India. His note from the guesthouse is somewhat demanding of Aziz; later, when Fielding and Aziz meet at the shrine, the Englishman continues to ask for comforts and privileges during his visit.

Though two years have passed since Part II, we see that Aziz is still extremely bitter about his arrest—and that it still plagues his reputation in British India. However, Forster also suggests, through a series of images of prisoners being freed, that Aziz's bitterness soon may be partially relieved. Chapter XXXV opens with the story of a Muslim saint whose great deed was to free all the prisoners in the old fort at Mau, and who died while doing so. When Aziz takes his children to visit part of the shrine to this saint, they pass a row of prisoners, one of whom will be freed during the Hindu procession of the Chief God that evening. These optimistic images in the chapter suggest that, although Aziz still identifies himself with prisoners, he too will soon be freed of his symbolic prison—his bitterness about Adela's accusation.

The emphasis on rebirth in Part III reinforces and deepens this sense of optimism. The Hindu celebration that provides the backdrop of the section is a celebration of the birth of the god Krishna. Furthermore, Part III takes place at the beginning of the rainy season, the time after the blistering hot season that brings extraordinary rains to nurture new crops. Aziz himself can be seen as a manifestation of rebirth, as his children are now living with him, and he seems to be focused on their education and upbringing. All of Aziz's hopes for a new India are invested in this younger generation.

Aziz, in a moment that epitomizes his character, feels torn between several different emotions upon learning that Fielding has actually married Stella Moore, not Adela Quested. In quick succession, Aziz feels embarrassed, then elated, then angry and prideful, then excited. Aziz's pride in himself and his behavior battle with his relief and his affection for Fielding; his anger at the name "Ronny Heaslop" battles with his love for the name "Mrs. Moore." Typically, Aziz intends for Fielding to take his words not literally, but as a performance of the emotions behind them. Indeed, though Aziz exhorts Fielding not to visit him while in Mau, several hours later, in the next chapter, Aziz himself rides over to the guesthouse and is disappointed to find that Fielding is not in. This confrontation between literal and figurative meaning that has been at the heart of the conflicts in the novel thus far continues to play a part here in the final chapters of the novel.

PART III, CHAPTERS XXXVI–XXXVII

SUMMARY: CHAPTER XXXVI

At sundown that day, Aziz remembers that he promised to send ointment over to the guesthouse to treat Fielding's brother-in-law's bee stings. Aziz procures some of Mohammed Latif's ointment and decides to take it over himself, as an excuse for a ride.

Outside, the Procession of the God is about to begin. The two claimants to the Rajah's throne, sensing that the Rajah might be dead, have arrived at the palace, but they make no moves toward the throne while the festival continues. Aziz runs into Godbole on the street and tells the professor the news about Fielding's wife. Godbole, however, has known all along that Fielding married Stella Moore, not Adela Quested. Aziz refrains from getting angry with Godbole out of respect for the festival time.

Riding toward the guesthouse, Aziz becomes cynical when he notices the English visitors out in the guesthouse boat watching the Hindu festival from afar. Aziz resents this sightseeing, which he views as really a form of ruling or patrolling India. Aziz rides on to the guesthouse, which is guarded only by a sleeping sentry. He lets himself in and snoops around the rooms, finally finding and reading a letter from Heaslop to Fielding and a letter from Adela to Stella. Aziz resents the intimate tone of the letters.

Frustrated, Aziz strikes the piano in front of him. Hearing the noise, Ralph Moore comes in, startled. Aziz recovers from his surprise and briskly asks to see the Englishman's bee stings. Ralph retreats from Aziz, saying that Aziz's hands are unkind. Ralph asks why Aziz is treating him and the other English visitors so cruelly. Aziz mentions Adela, but the procession outside nears the jail, and an outburst of sorrow from the crowd distracts them both.

Aziz decides to leave and shakes Ralph's hand absentmindedly. Aziz suddenly senses that Ralph is no longer afraid of him. Aziz asks Ralph if he can always tell when a stranger is his friend. Ralph says yes, he can. Aziz pronounces Ralph an Oriental, then shivers, remembering that he once said those exact words to Mrs. Moore in the mosque. Aziz is wary that a cycle is beginning again—the friendship of the mosque, followed by the horror of the caves. Aziz impulsively offers to take Ralph out on the water for a few minutes.

Once on the water, Aziz's old hospitality returns, and he begins to speak colorfully about the Hindu celebration. Ralph points out what looks like the Rajah floating on the water. Aziz admits that he does not know what it is, though he suspects it is the image of the old Rajah, which can be seen from only one point on the water. Aziz suddenly feels more like the visitor than the guide.

Ralph asks Aziz to row to a vantage point closer to the Procession of the God, in which rockets and guns are being shot off. Aziz is afraid of disturbing the celebration, and indeed, Godbole catches sight of them and begins to wave his arms wildly. Suddenly, Aziz's boat collides with Fielding's boat. Stella throws herself toward Fielding, and then forward toward Aziz. All four of them fall into the warm, shallow water, just as the Hindu festival, in the water nearby, reaches its climax. Their bodies, the props of the Hindu ceremony, Ronny's and Adela's letters, and the oars all swirl together.

Summary: Chapter XXXVII

After the boating accident, Aziz and Fielding suddenly revert to their old friendship. They go for a ride in the jungles around Mau before Fielding's departure. They know they will never see each other again.

During the ride, Aziz gives Fielding a letter for Adela, thanking her for her brave action at the trial. Fielding questions Aziz about Hinduism, reluctantly admitting that Stella and Ralph appear strangely drawn to the religion and to Mau. Aziz, impatient with talk of Hinduism, changes the subject to politics. Aziz and Fielding differ more politically than ever before, though they speak about their opinions with trust. Fielding now believes that the Empire is necessary, and he cares less about how polite it is. Aziz, however, hates the Empire. He predicts that India will become its own nation in the next generation, at which time he and Fielding might finally be friends. The two men embrace, and Fielding asks why they cannot be friends now, as they both seem to want it. But the land and sky themselves seem to arise between Fielding and Aziz, declaring, "No, not yet."

ANALYSIS: CHAPTERS XXXVI–XXXVII

Aziz's interaction with Ralph Moore provides the catalyst for Aziz and Fielding to restore their old friendship. Throughout their interaction, the two men display a remarkable level of intuition regarding the sentiment and intent behind each other's words. Aziz is initially callous and dismissive of Ralph, but then Ralph confronts this coldness by accusing Aziz of having unkind hands. Ralph senses that Aziz's resentment is payback for the Indian's own mistreatment at the hands of the English. Ralph's intuition surprises Aziz and reminds him of Mrs. Moore. When Aziz lets his guard down a moment later, Ralph senses that Aziz is relenting. Aziz knows that Ralph is sympathetic to him, sensitive and aware of his feelings much as Mrs. Moore was. Indeed, in an uncanny moment, Aziz uses the same words he used toward Mrs. Moore in the mosque, pronouncing Ralph an Oriental. Aziz is aware that his words start a cycle over again, and he is wary of the fear and accusation that may again follow this initial friendliness. Yet Forster presents this cycle as potentially a new version of the old cycle, an improvement that will promote greater understanding and not necessarily end in disaster. Ralph Moore is not a carbon copy of Mrs. Moore, but a younger generation; Aziz lets his guard down not out of naïve goodwill, but conscious choice.

Almost as remarkable as the initial conciliation between Aziz and Ralph Moore is their sightseeing boat trip. Aziz initially expresses bitterness toward Fielding and his wife as typical English people who seek to rule India under the guise of exploring India. Yet just several minutes later, Aziz, in characteristically unpredictable fashion, invites Ralph to sightsee under his guidance, just as he invited Mrs. Moore and Adela to see the Marabar Caves under his guidance. In both cases, Aziz knows little about the territory he shows his visitors. The important difference between Mau and Marabar, however, is that Ralph is an active sightseer: he spots the mysterious and elusive image of the old Rajah—an image that Aziz himself has never seen before. For once, Aziz drops his guise of all-knowing guide, allowing himself to be a visitor and spectator in his own country. In this depiction Forster suggests that the only sound approach to India is for both the English and Indians to be active lookers and to accept that no single person owns the knowledge of the land.

While the Hindu festival of Krishna serves as one backdrop to Part III, the elderly Rajah's death serves as the secondary backdrop. As the Rajah's personal physician, Aziz knows of the leader's death; though Aziz attempts to keep it secret until after the festival, the rest of the royalty of Mau has begun to suspect it. The beginning of Chapter XXXVI informs us that the two claimants to the throne have gathered at the palace but will make no move toward the throne until the festival is over. The Rajah's death thus suggests a general turning point, a changing of rulers. The patient and selfless approach of the two claimants to the throne suggest that politics is most humane when subordinated to a benevolent, religious worldview. In the context of Aziz and Fielding's discussion of India's future, the changing of rulers in Mau portends a general change in India and suggests an ideal means of change.

If Forster is critical of the British in Part I and the first half of Part II, and critical of Indians in the second half of Part II, in Part III he suggests that Hinduism holds the key by which all inhabitants of India might improve themselves and their country. In Part III, the larger concern of *A Passage to India*, centering on India's dilemma and future, moves beyond the personal level on which the novel's drama has played out—the friendship between Fielding and Aziz. For we see in Chapter XXXVII that neither Fielding nor Aziz has any patience for Hinduism. Fielding is still an atheist, and he resents the mysticism of his wife and brother-in-law. Aziz, though now more affectionate with Hindus, still ignores their practices and considers them silly and provincial. Stella and Ralph Moore, like their mother before them, are the characters most open to and interested in Hinduism. Through these two, the pain of Marabar is erased and potentially replaced by a collective vision. First, Ralph Moore connects with Aziz, and then Stella Moore—through her lunge towards him during the boating accident—symbolically reaches out to Aziz as well. It is through the Moores, and not Aziz and Fielding, that Forster expresses optimism in Part III.

Accordingly, the novel's final scene—featuring only Aziz and Fielding—betrays a realistic pessimism that is not present in the rest of Part III. Aziz and Fielding are happily back to their old selves, but these old selves suffer from drawbacks, new and old. Fielding has become more of a typical Englishman, more supportive of the British Empire than respectful of individual interactions. Likewise, Aziz's affectionate side has given way somewhat to a hardened pride in himself and his country.

The final message of *A Passage to India* is that though Aziz and Fielding want to be friends, both their personal histories and historical circumstances—as embodied by the Indian landscape—prevent their friendship. Forster's message has shifted throughout the course of the novel. At the start of the novel, characters such as Fielding and Aziz are evidence of Forster's faith in liberal humanism—the belief that with goodwill, intelligence, and respect, all individuals can connect and make a successful world. Yet here in the final scenes, the natural landscape of India itself seems to rise up and divide Aziz and Fielding from each other. Forster suggests that though men may be well intentioned, outside circumstances such as cultural difference, natural environment, and the interference of others can conspire to prevent their union. The final lines are pessimistic in this regard, but Forster does ultimately leave open the possibility that cross-cultural friendship, though elusive at the present moment, may be viable in the future. He implies that the combination of a respect for people as individuals and a belief in sameness and the unity of man—though sometimes a fearful notion, as Mrs. Moore has seen in the Marabar Caves—is the path most likely to lead to the openness and understanding that Aziz and Fielding seek.

Important Quotations Explained

1. In every remark [Aziz] found a meaning, but not
    always the true meaning, and his life though vivid was
    largely a dream.

This quotation occurs in Chapter VII during Aziz and Fielding's first meeting at Fielding's house, just before the tea party. Fielding has just made a brief comment in which he meant that the post-impressionist school of painting, to which Aziz has just made joking reference, is obscure and silly. Aziz, however, takes Fielding's comment to mean that it is silly for Aziz to have Western cultural knowledge. Aziz's embarrassment and discontent does not last long in this instance, but the incident foreshadows the misunderstandings that eventually break down the men's friendship.

Aziz's capacity for imagination and intuition leads him to genuine and deep friendships with Mrs. Moore and Fielding. However, Forster also shows that Aziz's intuition, which lacks grounding in fact, can lead him astray. In the aftermath of his trial, Aziz's false hunch that Fielding is courting Adela Quested leads to the breakdown of the men's relationship. In the above quotation, an early case of this false intuition, we see that Forster lays the blame for the breakdown on Aziz. Forster does not fault the difficulties of cross-cultural interaction, but rather Aziz's overactive imagination.

This flaw in Aziz's character, in a sense, also stands for a flaw of India itself. Forster presents Aziz's attitudes toward others as unfounded in reality. Cut off from a logical cause, Aziz's responses damage relationships rather than build them. This cut-off quality is later mirrored in the very landscape of India: the land around the Marabar Caves, described in Chapter XIV, appears "cut off at its root" and "infected with illusion." Forster presents India and Aziz as somewhat threatening to the logical and reasonable apprehension and reaction to reality that the author sees as epitomized by Western order.

This type of narrative comment that diagnoses Aziz's character is characteristic of Forster's writing. The author is concerned with presenting actions and dialogue, but he also seeks to draw comparisons and distinctions, to categorize and characterize. Indeed, Forster tells and comments as much as he shows. Still, not all of Forster's narrative diagnoses can be taken as absolute truth that stands throughout the novel. Though Forster depicts Aziz's imaginativeness as a handicap here, in other scenes we see that Forster values it.

2. Fielding did not even want to [correct Aziz]; he had dulled his craving for verbal truth and cared chiefly for truth of mood. As for Miss Quested, she accepted everything Aziz said as true verbally. In her ignorance, she regarded him as "India," and never surmised that his outlook was limited and his method inaccurate, and that no one is India.

This passage, occurring at Fielding's tea party later in Chapter VII, highlights a major distinction between the English and the Indians. Forster shows that Indians value the emotion and purpose behind a statement more than the literal words being stated. Indeed, we see that Aziz often tells lies—or, at least, lies by English standards—that are nonetheless truthful to Aziz himself because they reflect his desire to be hospitable, or because they serve to keep a conversation progressing smoothly. Similarly, other Indians, such as the Nawab Bahadur, give elaborate speeches that seem to have no coherent point, but that serve to rescue the other party from disgrace or impoliteness. Whereas the Indians seem to favor indirect speech, the English value statements primarily on the basis of literal truth. The English are incapable of intuiting the larger purpose or underlying tone behind a speech. Fielding's ability, as seen in this quotation, to respect statements for their mood as well as their truth, shows that he has learned cross-cultural lessons and can interact with Indians on their own standards, rather than his own.

This passage also highlights a problem with Adela's approach to India. Adela is still caught up with English literalism, even though she is well meaning and her intelligent individualism sets her apart from the rest of the English. Without a capacity for sympathy or affectionate understanding, Adela cannot realize that she is evaluating Indians on her own terms, rather than their terms. Adela's relationship with Aziz is, in this sense, without understanding or compassion. Rather, it is somewhat materialistic—Adela wants to know the "real India," and she expects Aziz to render it for her. This goal in itself is Adela's second mistake: whereas she seeks a single India, the real India exists in hundreds of guises, and no single Indian can offer an entire sense of it.

3.   [Mrs. Moore] felt increasingly (vision or nightmare?) that, though people are important, the relations between them are not, and that in particular too much fuss has been made over marriage.

This quotation, appearing in Chapter XIV during the train ride to the Marabar Caves, foreshadows Mrs. Moore's upcoming crisis with the cave echo. Ever since setting foot in India—or, more specifically, since hearing Godbole's religious song in Chapter VII—Mrs. Moore has felt a spiritual presence larger than her own Christian God. The largeness of this presence frightens Mrs. Moore and convinces her that human interactions are petty and meaningless. Her crisis at Marabar reinforces this feeling and leads her to paralyzing apathy. Mrs. Moore's vision, which shows that something larger than man encompasses the entire world and renders it equal, is a sort of negative version of Godbole's Hindu vision. The Hindu vision of the oneness of all living things finds comfort and joy in surrendering individual existence to the collective. Though Mrs. Moore takes this vision of impersonality to mean that human relationships are meaningless, the vision can also be liberating. Indeed, it is through a similar vision of impersonality that Adela is able to realize that Aziz is innocent and that she must proclaim him so, regardless of the cost to her own person and reputation.

This passage also evinces Forster's subtle critique of the institution of marriage. Mrs. Moore and Fielding, both potential mouthpieces for Forster himself, express distaste for marriage, specifically because it does not lead to a fruitful relationship that enlightens one about oneself or others. Few marriages exist in *A Passage to India*; indeed, we witness the breakdown of two—Ronny and Adela's before it even starts, and the McBrydes' through adultery. As such, Forster implies that the English sentimentalize the domestic structure of husband, wife, and children. They view this structure as a sacred symbol of all that is good about the British Empire, though the author contends that, in reality, domestic situations can lead to trouble and ignorance.

4.   "Your emotions never seem in proportion to their
objects, Aziz."
      "Is emotion a sack of potatoes, so much the pound, to
be measured out? Am I a machine?"

This exchange occurs in Chapter XXVII, as Aziz and Fielding's relationship begins to break down in the face of Fielding's new respect
and advocacy for Adela. Though Aziz and Fielding have several misunderstandings during this time, their main conflict centers on the
issue of reparation money from Adela. Aziz seeks damages from
Adela in the aftermath of the trial, but Fielding believes that Adela
should be given some credit for her bravery, rather than ruined
financially. Fielding points out that Aziz loves Mrs. Moore, who has
done nothing for Aziz, but begrudges Adela even after she has risked
her own reputation and marriage to eventually pronounce Aziz
innocent. Aziz and Fielding's disagreement over this issue demon-
strates the larger disparity between their worldviews. Fielding, who
values logic and reason, sees Aziz as fickle and irrational because he
bases his feelings on intuitions and connections that Fielding cannot
see or understand. Aziz, conversely, sees Fielding as succumbing to
the materialism and literalism of the rest of the English. The two
men often have lively conversations, but this quotation shows one
new trend in their discussions: they directly disagree with each other
and say so. Notably, Fielding is often the one who initially expresses
dissatisfaction with Aziz's behavior or opinions. Fielding becomes
more judgmental and less patient in the aftermath of the trial.

      This quotation also highlights the larger issue of British rule over
India. Britain's control of India began initially as a capitalist venture
with the British East India Company. As such, Britain appears to see
itself as taking the muddle and inefficiency of India and turning it
into an orderly, profitable, capitalist system. Aziz objects to this
kind of materialism, believing it values profit and efficiency over
intangible matters of spirit and love.

5. Were there worlds beyond which they could never touch, or did all that is possible enter their consciousness? They could not tell. . . . Perhaps life is a mystery, not a muddle. . . . Perhaps the hundred Indias which fuss and squabble so tiresomely are one, and the universe they mirror is one. They had not the apparatus for judging.

In this quotation from Chapter XXIX, which details Fielding's and Adela's reactions to Adela's strange experience at Marabar, Forster shows the inadequacy of English rationalism to evaluate mystical India. Adela is unable to articulate her frightening experience in the caves, even after her vision at the trial shows her Aziz's innocence. She and Fielding both approach the problem logically, attempting to outline a number of possible explanations: hallucination, the absence of the guide, and so on. Though Adela and Fielding are committed to rationally explaining the occurrence, each of their explanations falls short of Adela's experience. Here, we begin to see that Adela's experience in the cave stands as a sort of synecdoche—a metaphor that takes a part for the whole—for the entire experience of the foreignness of India. Like Marabar, India presents a confused set of stimulants, not all of which can be incorporated into a dominant explanation or interpretation. The only possible way to understand and classify the chaos of Marabar and India is to ascribe these mysteries to a force larger than humanity—a mystical force. Once mysticism is acknowledged, the "muddle" of Marabar becomes a "mystery," and the strangeness of India comes to appear as a coherent whole.

This passage also shows Fielding and Aziz coming closer to each other through mutual respect and similar experience. Though Fielding does not like Adela for much of the novel, disagreeing with her theoretical and unemotional approach to Indians and India, the two do share a level of rationalism and non-spiritualism. Both are atheists in a way and cannot truly fathom mystical presence as Mrs. Moore can. Fielding begins to respect Adela for her frank objectivity and her willingness to admit that she is unable to explain what happened in the caves. Through conversations like this one, Adela and Fielding grow closer by acknowledging the strangeness of the India around them. Aziz senses that this is the tenor of Adela and Fielding's friendship, and he begins to resent Fielding for it.

KEY FACTS

FULL TITLE
A Passage to India

AUTHOR
E.M. Forster

TYPE OF WORK
Novel

GENRE
Modernist novel; psychological novel

LANGUAGE
English

TIME AND PLACE WRITTEN
1912–1924; India, England

DATE OF FIRST PUBLICATION
1924

PUBLISHER
Edward Arnold

NARRATOR
Forster uses an unnamed third-person narrator

POINT OF VIEW
The third-person narrator is omniscient, attuned both to the physical world and the inner states of the characters

TONE
Forster's tone is often poetic and sometimes ironic or philosophical

TENSE
Immediate past

SETTING (TIME)
1910s or 1920s

SETTING (PLACE)
India, specifically the cities of Chandrapore and Mau

PROTAGONIST
Dr. Aziz

MAJOR CONFLICT
Adela Quested accuses Dr. Aziz of attempting to sexually assault her in one of the Marabar Caves. Aziz suspects Fielding has plotted against him with the English.

RISING ACTION
Adela Quested and Mrs. Moore's arrival in India; the women's befriending of Aziz; Adela's reluctant engagement to Ronny Heaslop; Ronny and the other Englishmen's disapproval of the women's interaction with Indians; Aziz's organization of an outing to the Marabar Caves for his English friends; Adela's and Mrs. Moore's harrowing experiences in the caves; Adela's public insinuation that Aziz assaulted her in the caves; the inflammation of racial tensions between the Indians and English in Chandrapore

CLIMAX
Aziz's trial; Adela's final admission that she is mistaken in her accusations and that Aziz is innocent; the courtroom's eruption; Aziz's release; the English community's rejection of Adela

FALLING ACTION
Fielding's conversations with Adela; Fielding and Aziz's bickering over Aziz's desire for reparations from Adela; Aziz's assumption that Fielding has betrayed him and will marry Adela; Aziz's increasingly anti-British sentiment; Fielding's visit to Aziz with his new wife, Stella; Aziz's befriending of Ralph and forgiveness of Fielding

THEMES
The difficulty of English-Indian friendship; the unity of all living things; the "muddle" of India; the negligence of British colonial government

MOTIFS
The echo; Eastern and Western architecture; Godbole's song

SYMBOLS
The Marabar Caves; the green bird; the wasp

FORESHADOWING
Adela's concern about breaking down during the trial; Fielding's interest in Hinduism at the end of Part II

KEY FACTS

Study Questions & Essay Topics

Study Questions

1. *What do Adela and Mrs. Moore hope to get out of their visit to India? Do they succeed?*

From the outset, both Mrs. Moore and Adela assert that their desire is to see the "real India" while they are in the country. Both women are frustrated with the lack of interaction between the English and the Indians, and they hope to get an authentic view of India rather than the standard tour for visiting colonials. Of the two, Mrs. Moore is less vocal than Adela in her impatience to discover the spirit of India, and she seems to be provisionally more successful in her goal. While Adela mopes in the Chandrapore Club, Mrs. Moore is already out on her own meeting Aziz in the mosque. Mrs. Moore, it seems, gets closer to a real sense of India because she seeks it out within Indians themselves, approaching them with sincere sympathy and interest. She does not desire to learn facts about Indian culture, but to forge a personal, individual connection. Adela, on the other hand, does not look to Indians for a glimpse of the "real India." Instead, she operates in a somewhat academic vein, going around and trying to gather information and impressions of the country. Adela wishes to get in contact with the "spirit" behind the "frieze" of India, but she skips the step in between. Rather than regard Indians as people like herself, she seems to view them as subjects for intellectual study.

Ultimately, both women largely fail in their quest to see the "real India." Adela is thwarted before she even begins: her engagement to Ronny forces her to give up her quest for communion with India and to take her place among the ranks of the rest of the Englishwomen in Chandrapore. Mrs. Moore, at least, realizes her mistaken quest before leaving India. On her train ride back to the coast to catch a return ship to England, Mrs. Moore begins to understand that she and Adela have both been misguided in their search for a single India. Mrs. Moore realizes that India exists in hundreds of ways and that it cannot be fathomed by a single mind or in a single visit.

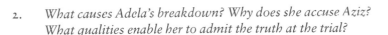

2.   *What causes Adela's breakdown? Why does she accuse Aziz?*
       What qualities enable her to admit the truth at the trial?

Adela is an intelligent and inquisitive girl, but she has a limited worldview, and is, as Fielding puts it, a "prig." Adela has come to India to experience an adventure and to gauge her desire to marry Ronny. During the early stages of the visit, she weighs both her emotions and her experiences with an almost clinical precision. Adela wants to see the "real India," which apparently means an India unfiltered through the lens of English people and colonial institutions. But in her desire to have a single authentic experience and a single authentic understanding of India, Adela is unable to take in the complexity of her surroundings, which have been muddled even further by the presence of the English. There is no real India; there are a hundred real Indias. But Adela's attempt to make her Indian experience match her comfortable preconceptions cannot prepare her for this fact. As the muddle of India slowly works its way into her mind, it undermines her preconceptions without giving her anything with which to replace them.

On the way to the Marabar Caves, Adela realizes for the first time that she does not love Ronny. The sheer incomprehensibility of experience—as represented by the echo in the caves—overwhelms her for the first time. Traumatized, Adela feels not only as though her world is breaking down, but as though India itself is responsible for the breakdown. This idea solidifies in her mind as the idea that Aziz, an Indian, has attacked and attempted to rape her. Still, Adela is committed to the truth and has a strong mind. When she sees Aziz at the trial, she reenters the scene in her mind in a sort of disembodied vision. She realizes that her actions are ruining a real person's life, and she is therefore able to pull back and withdraw her charge before a verdict can be handed down.

3.   *What purpose does Part III, "Temple," play in* A Passage
       to India?

The first issue that Forster addresses in *A Passage to India* is whether or not an Englishman and an Indian can be friends. Parts I and II of the novel depict the friendship of Aziz and Fielding, first on the ascendant, and then as it breaks apart. Part II leaves us with a pessimistic sense that cross-cultural communication is futile, and that such friendships cause more hurt than good. Part III, however, gives us a measured resolution to this issue. In this final section of the novel, Fielding and Aziz meet again after two years and resolve their misunderstandings—though not their differences. Forster shows that while outside forces can make cross-cultural friendships nearly impossible, the friendships themselves, whether successful or not, are still a valuable experience. The pessimistic ending of Part II is thus tempered by Forster's depiction of Aziz and Fielding in Part III.

Additionally, Forster uses Part III to address the issue of how a foreigner can best understand and make peace with the "muddle" of India. Throughout Parts I and II, Forster shows several main characters—Mrs. Moore, Adela, Fielding—experiencing spiritual crises in the face of the chaos of Indian experience. Part III, which is set in the Hindu state of Mau during a Hindu religious festival, offers the Hindu vision of the oneness of all living things as a possible answer to the problem of comprehending India. The most mystical characters of the novel take the spotlight in Part III. Godbole serves in Mau as an educator and religious figure, and Mrs. Moore reappears through her two children, Ralph and Stella. If Forster is pessimistic about Fielding and Aziz's friendship, in Part III he at least offers the collectivity of Hindu love as a potential source of hope and redeeming possibility.

SUGGESTED ESSAY TOPICS

1. What is Forster's primary critique of the British in India? What does he appear to think of the Empire in general?

2. Evaluate the role of negation in the novel. Look for instances of the word "nothing," descriptions that use lack or negativity, and plot points in which "nothing" happens, though characters think something does happen. What does negation signify and how is it used?

3. What is the role of nature in *A Passage to India*?

4. What part does sexuality play in the novel? Consider any differences of opinion about sexuality between Fielding and Aziz and between Ronny and Adela.

5. Compare Forster's depiction of the English in Chandrapore with his depiction of Aziz's Indian community. Do the two groups have any similarities? Does Forster portray one group more sympathetically?

REVIEW & RESOURCES

QUIZ

1. In the opening dialogue of the novel, who is most open to the possibility of Indian-English friendship?

   A. Hamidullah
   B. Aziz
   C. Mahmoud Ali
   D. Hamidullah's wife

2. Why is Aziz at the mosque where he meets Mrs. Moore?

   A. Because it is the traditional time for prayer
   B. Because Englishwomen have stolen his tonga
   C. Because he is restless and agitated
   D. Because he sensed her presence

3. How does Aziz sense Mrs. Moore is sympathetic to him?

   A. She is knowledgeable about Islam
   B. She approaches him first
   C. She appears unafraid of him
   D. She speaks frankly about her dislike for Mrs. Turton

4. Why, at the beginning of the novel, is Adela Quested dissatisfied with her visit to India?

   A. Because she wants to be engaged to Ronny
   B. Because she wants to see the real India
   C. Because she does not get along with Mrs. Moore
   D. Because she dislikes Ronny's friends

5. Why does Turton throw the Bridge Party?

   A. He throws one every year
   B. Because his superior ordered him to
   C. To please Adela
   D. To please the Nawab Bahadur

6. Who runs their horse into the flowers at the Bridge Party?

    A. Miss Derek
    B. Aziz
    C. Panna Lal
    D. The Bhattacharyas

7. What is the main reason Aziz decides not to attend the Bridge Party?

    A. It coincides with the anniversary of his wife's death
    B. He feels sick to his stomach
    C. He wants to spend time with his children
    D. He is angry with Major Callendar

8. What disconcerts Ronny about his mother's story about meeting a young man in the mosque?

    A. She disobeyed his orders
    B. She should not be hanging around with younger men
    C. Her tone of voice does not indicate that the young man is Indian
    D. She sounds depressed

9. Which of the following does *not* upset Mrs. Moore on the day of Fielding's tea party?

    A. Adela and Ronny's bickering
    B. Aziz's overfriendliness
    C. Adela's spontaneous admission that she will return to England
    D. Godbole's religious song

10. Which of the following does *not* cause Adela to change her mind and become engaged to Ronny?

    A. The landscape and sky of Chandrapore
    B. The sexual magnetism between her and Ronny
    C. Her and Ronny's mutual distaste for Miss Derek and the Nawab Bahadur
    D. A brief lecture from Mrs. Moore

11. How does Fielding shock the Indians in Aziz's sickroom?

    A. He is bluntly honest
    B. He sits on the floor
    C. He hugs Aziz
    D. He denounces Islam

12. How does Aziz show Fielding that he considers Fielding like a brother to him?

    A. He lets Fielding sit on his floor
    B. He gossips about the Turtons
    C. He shows Fielding a picture of his wife
    D. He tells Fielding the names of his children

13. What event, prior to the visit to the caves, prompts Adela's and Mrs. Moore's feelings of emotional emptiness?

    A. Their arrival in India
    B. Adela's engagement
    C. The production of *Cousin Kate*
    D. Godbole's song

14. Which of the following does *not* disturb Mrs. Moore in the Marabar Caves?

    A. The echo
    B. The religious singing
    C. A baby's hand
    D. The crowd

15. What makes Fielding suspicious during the trip to the caves?

    A. Adela's hasty departure
    B. Aziz's overexcited demeanor
    C. Mrs. Moore's apathy
    D. The absence of Adela's servant

16. Why does McBryde believe that Indians are criminal?

    A. Because the English treat them poorly
    B. Because they are inherently evil
    C. Because of the Indian climate
    D. Because they are greedy and crime pays

17.   What does Fielding do that angers the members of the Englishmen's club?

    A.   He hangs around with Aziz
    B.   He pronounces Aziz innocent
    C.   He fights with a soldier
    D.   He does not stand when Ronny enters

18.   What prompts Adela to suddenly proclaim Aziz innocent?

    A.   She feels incredibly guilty
    B.   She finally believes Mrs. Moore's assertion that Aziz is a good man
    C.   She has a vision of Marabar and sees that Aziz was not in the cave with her
    D.   She becomes intimidated by Aziz's lawyer

19.   Why is Aziz upset during his own victory celebration?

    A.   Because Fielding leaves with Adela
    B.   Because he has been hardened by prison
    C.   Because his friends are threatening the English
    D.   Because he knows the English will regard him as guilty regardless of the verdict

20.   Why is Fielding upset with Aziz after the trial?

    A.   Because Aziz makes himself look guilty
    B.   Because Aziz refuses to credit Adela's bravery at the trial
    C.   Because Aziz tries to loot the hospital
    D.   Because Aziz quits his job

21.   In which European country does Fielding stop and admire the architecture on the way back to England?

    A.   France
    B.   Spain
    C.   Italy
    D.   Greece

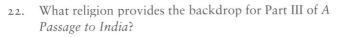

22. What religion provides the backdrop for Part III of *A Passage to India*?

   A. Hinduism
   B. Islam
   C. Buddhism
   D. Sikhism

23. With what character is this religion associated?

   A. Aziz
   B. Fielding
   C. Mahmoud Ali
   D. Godbole

24. Through which character does Aziz renew his friendship with Fielding?

   A. Stella Moore
   B. Ralph Moore
   C. His oldest son
   D. Godbole

25. Which of the following is *not* a title of one of the three parts of *A Passage to India*?

   A. "Mosque"
   B. "Temple"
   C. "Cave"
   D. "Festival"

ANSWER KEY:

1: A; 2: B; 3: D; 4: B; 5: C; 6: C; 7: A; 8: C; 9: B; 10: D; 11: A; 12: C; 13: D; 14: B; 15: A; 16: C; 17: D; 18: C; 19: A; 20: B; 21: C; 22: A; 23: D; 24: B; 25: D

Suggestions for Further Reading

BEER, JOHN. A PASSAGE TO INDIA: *Essays in Interpretation.* Totowa, New Jersey: Barnes & Noble Books, 1986.

BRADBURY, MALCOLM, ed. *E.M. Forster,* A PASSAGE TO INDIA: *A Casebook.* London: Macmillan, 1970.

FORSTER, E.M. *Aspects of the Novel.* New York: Harcourt, Brace & World, 1954.

GANGULY, ADWAITA P. *India, Mystic, Complex, and Real: A Detailed Study of E.M. Forster's* A PASSAGE TO INDIA. Delhi: Motilal Banarsidass Publishers, 1990.

GARDNER, PHILIP. *E.M. Forster: The Critical Heritage.* London: Routledge, 1997.

HERZ, JUDITH SCHERER. A PASSAGE TO INDIA: *Nation and Narration.* New York: Twayne Publishers, 1993.

KIPLING, RUDYARD. *Kim.* New York: Penguin Classics, 1987.

LAGO, MARY. *E.M. Forster: A Literary Life.* New York: St. Martin's Press, 1995.

MAY, BRIAN. *The Modernist as Pragmatist: E.M. Forster and the Fate of Liberalism.* Columbia: University of Missouri Press, 1997.

SAID, EDWARD W. *Orientalism.* New York: Random House, 1979.

STONE, WILFRED. *The Cave and the Mountain: A Study of E.M. Forster.* Palo Alto, California: Stanford University Press, 1966.

WILDE, ALAN. *Art and Order: A Study of E.M. Forster.* New York: New York University Press, 1964.